D0684404

Judaism—
An Eternal Covenant

HOWARD R. GREENSTEIN

Judaism— An Eternal Covenant

Wipf & Stock
PUBLISHERS
Eugene, Oregon

Wipf and Stock Publishers
199 W 8th Ave, Suite 3
Eugene, OR 97401

Judaism
An Eternal Covenant
By Greenstein, Howard R.

ISBN: 1-59752-714-9
Publication date 5/30/2006
Previously published by Fortress Press, 1983

To Lenore
My partner with God
in an eternal covenant of our very own

Contents

Foreword

As the editor of a triad of books about three of America's major religious faiths, Judaism, Catholicism, and Protestantism, I welcome the first in the series, *Judaism—An Eternal Covenant* by Howard R. Greenstein. This volume is to be followed by *A Catholic Vision* by Stephen Happel and David Tracy, and by *Protestantism—Its Modern Meaning,* now being prepared by an eminent historian and churchman.

Judaism—An Eternal Covenant, written for both Jews and non-Jews, is designed to answer questions that are frequently asked about this major religious orientation:

What is Judaism?

Whence did it come?

What are its major beliefs and customs?

What are its holy days and holidays, and what do they signify?

Why is Judaism of such importance today?

From long and careful study Dr. Greenstein provides answers to these and many other important questions. As a clergyman and university professor, as a lecturer and writer, he brings to these pages the distillation of many years of research and reflection.

He notes that Judaism is the wellspring of the most honored and civilizing ideals in the history of humankind and lies, therefore, at the epicenter of our Western culture. Judaism's unique achievements consist not only in forging and maintaining the first monotheism on the face of the earth, but also in emphasizing the worth and the dignity of every human being and giving prime value to freedom, justice, and equality. In these contributions, over a period of history numbering thirty-five hundred or perhaps even four thousand years, Judaism has made available matchless gifts to both Christendom and Islam. Both Christianity and Islam are indebted to Judaism for the Hebrew Scriptures from which each has drawn heavily for inspiration, morality, and historical drama.

Today, Judaism has a more profound meaning and influence on millions of people than perhaps at any time in its history, more significant and powerful than even in the days of the psalmists and the prophets, or the judges and the patriarchs. Dr. Greenstein inevitably focuses on two major events of the twentieth century: the tragic Holocaust of six million European Jews, put to death by Nazi Germany before and during World War II, and the establishment in 1948 of the new State of Israel, the third Jewish Commonwealth.

Howard R. Greenstein, a graduate of Cornell University, received his rabbinical ordination and a Master of Arts in Hebrew Letters at the Hebrew Union College—Jewish Institute of Religion in Cincinnati. He earned the degree of Doctor of Philosophy at Ohio State University, and his doctoral dissertation was of such excellence that it was subsequently published in 1981 in the Brown Judaic Studies of Scholars Press as *Turning Point: Zionism and Reform Judaism.*

Spring 1983 — Carl Hermann Voss

Introduction

> *Now therefore, if you will obey my voice and keep my covenant, you shall be my own possession among all peoples . . . and you shall be to me a kingdom of priests and a holy nation.*
>
> Exod. 19:5–6

Jews and Judaism are not easy to understand. If they were, a book like this would not be necessary. Even Jews find it difficult to understand themselves and each other. The tradition is ancient and many faceted, and it therefore invites variety in interpretation. From the very earliest sources of rabbinic literature, in the Talmud and elsewhere, Jewish learning and teaching thrived on debate and controversy. The sages taught that every argument deserved a hearing, for one could never know whether future generations might not discover truth in the minority view as well as in the majority.

Among non-Jews, of course, the confusion about Jewish belief and practice is even more widespread. On a recent trip to Europe, a non-Jewish traveling companion asked me if he might be allowed to visit our synagogue some Friday evening for a Sabbath service. I was astounded that anyone should even wonder whether such permission was necessary; but, as I learned, to many non-Jews Judaism is a religious "closed shop" with membership privileges limited to only a select circle called "the chosen people."

Membership in the Jewish community is indeed a matter of association with the chosen people, but that is by no means a matter of inheritance alone; nor does it preclude a warm and open welcome to non-Jews who seek not necessarily to join but at least to appreciate what the Jewish religion teaches, practices, and promotes.

This book is such a statement of welcome to Jews and non-Jews alike. Even though many Jews instinctively place their trust and confidence in Judaism, many more of them do not understand it any better than the vast majority of their non-Jewish neighbors. Many non-Jews may be vaguely aware that Christianity evolved in large measure from its roots in Judaism; but few can explain or understand the nature of those Jewish origins and the Jewish elements within Christianity. This volume is directed to both communities.

Judaism is primarily, though not exclusively, a religion. That makes it a difficult subject to discuss in contrast to other religions. It is virtually impossible to identify a "Christian atheist" because they are mutually exclusive terms. One cannot be a Christian if one is an atheist, and one certainly ceases to be an atheist if one is a Christian.

At the same time, one can and does speak of a "Jewish atheist." Indeed, the galaxy of Jewish genius across the centuries is filled with luminaries who categorically denied religious beliefs of any kind. These included some of the spokesmen for the nineteenth-century *Haskalah* ("Enlightenment"), leaders of various Jewish socialist movements in Eastern Europe, and even some founders of Zionism, the major expression of Jewish nationalism.

Many Jews reject the religious components of their identity but still maintain their loyalty to Jewish ideals and aspirations. What links them to their Jewish past and commits them to a Jewish future is not faith in a deity but their attachments to the Jewish people. Peoplehood is their strongest common denominator. Whatever a Jew may deny about religious claims, he will never repudiate his ties to other Jews and still assert himself to be a Jew. Being part of the Jewish people is where Judaism begins.

That is not, however, where Judaism ends. The Jewish people cannot be fully understood without reference to their religious roots. Everything they created, everything they cherished sprouted from spiritual seeds. Their language, their literature, their philosophy, their history, even their music, art, and poetry all originated and flourished in religious sources. It is impossible to appreciate Jewish culture without appreciating its spiritual context from the earliest past to the most immediate present.

The spiritual context of this Jewish cultural legacy is what Jews from earliest times conceived as "the Covenant." The Covenant is simply an agreement between God and the Jewish people, the basic requirements of which are fully explained in the Torah, the first five books of the Hebrew Scriptures. The Covenant stipulates that God will protect and prosper the Jewish people, if they in return will observe the statutes and injunctions which God commands. If they violate his commandments, God will punish them. That the community of Israel is party to this difficult and divine partnership confers upon it the distinction of being a chosen people. That "chosenness" implies primarily a heritage not of special privilege but of special responsibility; and this serves as a unique model, a high standard of divine truth and goodness.

The corollary of rewards for the observance of the Covenant, of course, is the penalties for its violation. God and the Jewish people are partners in the task of building a better world, and if Israel fails, all creation inevitably suffers.

The belief that God actually chose the Jewish people for this task is a matter of faith. History, however, confirms that Israel chose God in these terms. That truth is what matters most of all. The Jewish people have forever perceived themselves as living to serve the Supreme Creator and have ascribed meaning and significance to their own experience only as a consequence of this imperishable relationship.

Having entered into this binding Covenant, no Jew can shed its obligations. He may renounce them. He may even deny the deity. That explains how it is possible for him to be an atheistic Jew. The traditionalist may regard him as an erring or faithless Jew. Still, he is a Jew. The Covenant continues. Paul was so indoctrinated with this view as a Jew that he declared in his Epistle to the Romans: "the Jews are entrusted with the oracles of God. What if some were unfaithful? Does their faithlessness nullify the faithfulness of God? By no means!" (Rom. 3:2–4).

Judaism therefore is essentially an eternal Covenant. It is an irrevocable agreement which binds every Jew to God and to every generation of his people, past, present and future. That bond endures for the purpose of achieving all the greatness and goodness the soul can produce in consort with the source of all existence, which most

Jews call God. For those who have not experienced this Covenant, the concept is admittedly a difficult one. Those who have absorbed it, however, understand why its spokesmen have called it eternal.

As basic as this concept may be to a clear understanding of Jewish religion, the Covenant has never been a static notion either in its development or in its perception at any particular period. The prophetic notion in the later chapters of the Book of Isaiah, for example, that the God of Israel is the only God of all existence clearly did not emerge out of a cultural vacuum. It was the gradual consequence of centuries of experience and thoughtful reflection. Even more abstract is the later medieval, philosophical thesis that the infinite nature of God is impossible even to discuss except in negative attributes. Post-Holocaust literature, as we shall note, has altered this central concept of Covenant even further.

In its development and in the Jews' perception of it, the Covenant has been subject to continuous change and modification. The prophets strenuously challenged the populace over the relative priorities of the ritual law and moral law as requirements for the observance of the Covenant. The Pharisees repudiated the authority of the Sadducees on the basis of the Oral Law, which the latter excluded from the Covenant, since in their view it could include only the Written Law. Karaites in the ninth and tenth centuries later rejected the teachings of the Rabbinites. In the nineteenth century, Hasidim, in behalf of "inwardness" and transcendence, defied the denunciations of the more legalistic *Mitnagdim* ("adversaries"). The current diversity in thought and practice among Orthodox, Conservative, and Reform Jews in North America, as well as differences between Sephardic Jews and Ashkenazic Jews throughout the world, is more than ample evidence that perceptions of the Covenant between God and Israel have varied dramatically from time to time and from one community to another.

Even in the realm of particular ideological issues, Judaism has never been a monolithic faith. Variations in Jewish literature abound on the widest range of subjects, from beliefs about God and the origins of creation to speculation about the meaning of death and the existence of a world beyond the grave. Space simply does not permit an exhaustive explication of this diversity; in addition, to focus on such subtleties and distinctions might obscure rather than illumine the dominant themes of Jewish thought and observance. Although Judaism is itself a product of considerable tension and continuous dialectic, a number of prevailing motifs emerge out of Jewish experience which a student of this heritage can clearly recognize and affirm.

Regardless of this theological panorama, however, the prevailing unity of the Jewish people remains unchanged. In spite of existing differences, most Jews will agree on the shape if not the substance of the major components of that timeless Covenant between themselves and their Creator. More importantly, they will acknowledge its priority and its application in their own lives, however they may define it.

The meaning of that Covenant and the current multiplicity of its interpretations are the essence of this book. For Jew and non-Jew alike, mastering that subject is the key to an adequate understanding of Judaism and the Jewish people.

PART ONE

THE COMPONENTS

1
God

The foundation of all foundations, the pillar supporting all wisdoms, is the recognition of the reality of God.

Maimonides (1135-1204)

THE EXISTENCE OF GOD

The fundamental belief of the biblical faith that lies at the heart of Judaism is the premise that God is the source of all being. The ancient sages who formulated the basic precepts of Judaism assumed that the world could not have originated or endured without God.

The basic assumption that God is the source of all being is declared throughout the Bible. The very first verse of Genesis, for example, opens with a resounding affirmation: "In the beginning God created the heavens and the earth." The statement is not an inquiry about the existence of God. It is a proclamation, an affirmation.

Later in the Bible, the announcement by Moses of the Ten Commandments begins with a decisive pronouncement: "I am the Lord your God, Who brought you out of the land of Egypt, out of the house of bondage" (Exod. 20:2). The issue of God's existence is not an open question here. Redemption from oppression can only be the consequence of divine action.

Moses himself did not pause to cite any evidence to convince his people. In the words "'Hear, O Israel: The Lord our God is one Lord'" (Deut. 6:4), he was telling the people that although the essence of God may escape human understanding, His existence is beyond doubt or debate.

The same conviction of God's existence is expressed in the Book of Psalms. The psalms were the hymns of ancient Israel. These beautiful lyrics were written or composed by many individuals, although more than half are attributed to David. All the composers are known collectively as the Psalmist. Even the Psalmist declared that only "the fool hath said in his heart: 'There is no God'" (Ps. 14:1).

Although the Bible sometimes digresses into a brief attempt to demonstrate the greatness or majesty of God, invariably it is not so much an effort to prove that God exists as it is an assertion of what God's existence implies. This is seen in the first verse of Psalm 127: "Unless the Lord builds the house, those who build it labor in vain. Unless the Lord watches over the city, the watchman stays awake in vain." Later, the Psalmist inquires of God: "Whither shall I go from Thy spirit? Or whither shall I flee from Thy presence?" (Ps. 139:7). In both instances, the issue is not God's existence, but the inescapable consequences of an existence already assumed.

The existence of God was demonstrated in the extraordinary confrontation on Mt. Carmel between Elijah and the prophets of Baal. In 1 Kings 18, Elijah challenges the people to choose between God and Baal. Then by the ordeal of fire and water, Elijah demonstrates the supreme power of Israel's God. Yet this event was not so much a "proof" of the existence of God as it was a convincing manifestation of God in action.

During the Middle Ages, Judaism developed a pronounced inclination to devise philosophical proofs of the existence of God. Indeed, beginning with the tenth-century Jewish philosopher Saadia and continuing for centuries into modern times, Jewish scholars produced a vast literature of complicated and detailed arguments in defense of beliefs in a personal God. Although that intellectual legacy remains a major contribution to Jewish thought, it never became a doctrinal matter of Jewish faith.

Judaism teaches that neither logical arguments nor personal experience can totally explain being or encompass the nature of God. The mind of the finite creature that is man cannot envisage even the dimensions of infinite reality, much less its content. When Moses pleaded with God to disclose His true nature, God explained: "'You cannot see My face; for man shall not see Me and live'" (Exod. 33:20).

The prophet Isaiah emphasized the same limits to understanding of God: "My thoughts are not your thoughts, neither are your ways My ways, says the Lord" (Isa. 55:8).

Perhaps the most defiant challenge in the Bible to this inherent limitation of the human mind and spirit was Job's complaint about the injustice of God's decision to punish him. God pierces Job's haughtiness by asking him: "'Where were you when I laid the foundation of the earth? Tell Me, if you have understanding!'" (Job 38:4). Job is forced to concede: "I have uttered what I did not understand, things too wonderful for me, which I did not know" (Job 42:3).

The twelfth-century Jewish philosopher Maimonides insisted that trying to comprehend God adequately was so hopeless that it was impossible to describe Him in positive terms. Language could never convey what God was, only what He was not. According to Maimonides, any intelligent discussion about the nature of God could only contain negatives.

The consensus in Jewish literature is that the fullness of God is impossible to know. On a theoretical level, it is difficult to conceive how one portion of reality could possibly comprehend the ultimate source of all reality. The task is more than our limited minds can manage.

Even in the realm of ordinary events, countless mysteries in science and philosophy still defy explanation in terms of human experience. If we are so far from answers in the finite world, how immeasurable must the distance be even to touch the outer limits of God as the infinite reality. Astronomers tell us that we are unable to measure the farthest reaches of the universe, much less understand it. Microbiologists tell us that the inner world of organic matter may be equally inaccessible. If such be our human predicament, how can any intelligent being pretend to exhaust knowledge about the ultimate source of all being itself?

For Jews in search of God, intellectual humility is the first prerequisite. At the same time, the fact that we cannot know all truth does not condemn us seekers to concede failure from the outset. We can know at least part of the truth. Certainly, we can accumulate enough insight into the nature of God to understand what the world of moral obligations is about and something of what that world requires of us. Judaism teaches that what we know about God may best be explained by the term "ethical monotheism," which affirms that a single God is the source of all being and all moral action.

ETHICAL MONOTHEISM

Ethical monotheism is a uniquely Jewish religious concept which affirms that all existence was created and is governed by a single God. That Deity is also the source and the paradigm for moral action. This idea was a revolutionary development in the history of religions. Many knowledgeable students of religion maintain that this proposition is the greatest single contribution of Judaism to the spiritual heritage of Western civilization.

This extraordinary understanding of the nature of God rests upon an appreciation of its three major aspects. The first is the belief that God is one and not many. The ancient Jewish people, unlike their contemporaries, did not believe that the world was fragmented under the domain of several different gods. They posited the existence of only one Supreme Being who alone accounted for all the diversity in the universe. He was the Creator and Sustainer of all there is. The first hypothesis implies several corollaries which emphasize the uniqueness of this concept.

One entailed a belief that the unity of God encouraged much greater unity among the people who worshipped him. If people worshipped many gods, inevitably favorites would emerge among them and factions would develop; each would promote the supremacy of their own choice. Monotheism theoretically precludes such conflicts. "It shall come to pass in the latter days," declares Isaiah, "that the mountain of the house of the Lord shall be established as the highest of the mountains, . . . and many peoples shall come and say: 'Come, let us go up to the mountain of the Lord, to the house of the God of Jacob; that He may teach us His ways and that we may walk in His paths'" (Isa. 2:2–3). From its earliest beginnings, Judaism taught that the unity of mankind was a corollary of the belief in one God. That is clearly a distinctive quality of the concept of monotheism.

When Judaism proclaims that God is one, it means that He is not simply a numerical unity, but also a qualitative unity. That is the second major aspect of monotheism in Judaism. God is not only one; He is unique as the Source and Sustainer of all moral values. He is not only one unto Himself; He is the only one of His kind in the universe. There is no other "One" like God. During the Rabbinic period (200 Before the Common Era, or B.C.E.–500 Common Era, or C.E.), the Roman emperor often enjoyed the title of "king of kings." To emphasize the singularity of God, the rabbinic sages acclaimed God as "the King of the kings of kings."

To hold that God is the Source and Sustainer of moral values is to insist upon an objective status for ethical ideals. They are not the impulsive fabrication of human minds, but are rooted in the very structure of creation. Moral laws have objective validity similar to the laws of physics. They are not our inventions, but it is for us to discover them. Just as it would be foolish to defy the law of gravity, and hope to escape the consequences, so is it perilous to presume that a human infant could grow to emotional maturity without ever being loved or cared for. In both cases, the penalty for ignoring the law is a natural consequence of defying the existing realities of the universe. The uniqueness of God in this context is the complex but delicate blend of both physical and spiritual reality in a single deity which accounts for the balance, harmony, and order of nature within us and without.

The uniqueness of God, as Judaism has taught it, included still a third aspect which clearly set ancient Israel apart from all other peoples. Evidence abounds that from earliest times, God in Judaism was not simply the supreme moral authority, but the supreme moral agent. Just as God limited His range of operations by imposing particular moral laws, His credibility henceforth would rest not only on legislating truth but on His being identified with truth. God could not violate either physical or moral laws without seriously compromising His integrity.

A biblical passage that clearly reflects this principle is the conversation between God and Abraham concerning the impending destruction of Sodom and Gomorrah (Gen. 18:17–33). God decides to disclose to Abraham His plans to destroy the two cities because of their flagrant transgressions of moral decency. Abraham, however, objects to such a decision that would indiscriminately obliterate the innocent with the guilty, and calls God to account on the basis of His own ethical standards.

"Wilt Thou indeed," asks Abraham, "destroy the righteous with the wicked?" He then proceeds to negotiate with God on behalf of the innocent. He begins by speculating whether there may be as few as fifty righteous people in the cities. Would that not be sufficient to annul the decree? God concedes that Abraham's argument is legitimate. He agrees that for the sake of fifty righteous people the cities will be saved if Abraham can find them. Abraham proceeds to inquire for the sake of forty, then thirty, twenty, and finally just ten. In each case God is willing to alter his judgment if the innocent number can be found.

Eventually, not even ten innocent persons can be found, and God proceeds to destroy the cities. The point, however, is not Abraham's defeat but his acknowledged right to challenge God and hold Him personally accountable for the laws He has formulated.

That unique quality of monotheism in Judaism stands in sharp contrast to the prevailing belief of other cultures of the period. Greek mythology, and especially Greek tragedy, were rooted in a premise that, endowed with supreme power, the Olympian gods could manipulate their human subjects at will. However persistent or courageous an individual effort might be, the struggle was hopeless in the face of divine opposition. The gods were not subject to the same rules as ordinary mortals.

Monotheism reportedly existed also in Egypt prior to the time of the Exodus and Revelation at Sinai. The Pharaoh Ikhnaton in the fourteenth century B.C.E. postulated the existence of a single, all-powerful god that superseded all the lesser pagan gods of Egyptian mythology. That belief differed from its later transformation in Judaism, however, in at least three important respects.

First, Ikhnaton's monotheism remained ultimately a personal faith. It never fully succeeded in touching the soul of an entire people in service to the one-God concept as it later developed in Judaism.

Secondly, Ikhnaton's monotheism was not ethical. It did not include that unique quality which demanded divine observance of moral laws as well as human obedience. It did not even acknowledge the deity as the source of moral law, much less its primary agent.

And thirdly, the priests of the generation after Ikhnaton's death abandoned this new monotheism and restored the rejected polytheism.

As abstract as the concept of ethical monotheism might seem, the knowledge of God in Judaism has rested far more on experience than on theoretical speculation. Jews have always understood God in terms of His activity in the world and His involvement in human affairs. That experience extends to the realm of physical nature as well as human nature. The universe itself is evidence of God as the Creator of all that exists. He is the Meaning beyond the mystery of all existence. The cosmic and biological processes that exhibit order, interdependence, and unity everywhere reflect His creative will. God may be found in sunsets, the change of seasons, in an exploding galaxy, and in a blade of grass, but most of all in the moral order that man's nature requires for its maximum fulfillment. He not only initiated those processes; He alone sustains them and invites man to join Him in renewing those processes continually by their joint efforts.

At every major turning point in Israel's history, the Jewish people encountered God in a different context. In the event of the Exodus from Egypt, they discovered God as the sole protector and preserver of human freedom. He was the spark of inspiration that compelled them to break the chains of slavery and to risk their lives and their children's lives for the precious, inalienable right to liberty. Only God can confer such a blessing. No human agent can bestow it or deny it.

At Sinai, the Israelites envisaged God as the Lawgiver, the Source of every standard for justice, truth, and goodness. They discovered in their wilderness experience that the foundation of a stable society required rules that were rooted in some objective reality, not in the momentary impulse of popular fashion.

In their moments of trial and temptation, they found in God their Healer. In times of need, He became their Helper. In the unfolding of an endless series of significant events, they understood Him as the Author of history. Life was not a meaningless succession of unrelated accidents. The people of Israel assigned to their individual and collective lives a divine purpose that would ultimately lead to their own fulfillment and redemption.

Even in the face of total defeat, God was the Savior. For some people, the defeat might mean death, and the salvation some form of life beyond the grave. In a larger context, however, the defeat might pertain to ignorance, insensitivity, fear, or any other human limitation. The victories a person achieves over these disabilities are clearly for Judaism a form of salvation or healing. This healing is also a display of God's power as a personal Savior.

The limits of God's reality in the world are defined only by the limits of human experience. Judaism teaches that God relates to people in as many ways as people choose to relate to Him.

One of the outstanding intellectual contributors to the idea of ethical monotheism in Judaism was the spiritual giant of Hellenistic Judaism, the philosopher Philo (30 B.C.E.–45 C.E.). The influence of the traditional Jewish idea of God is clearly evident in the Philonic emphasis on God's transcendence and spirituality. The concept of God for Philo is elevated above all values and perfections conceivable to the human mind. God is above knowledge and virtue, even above the good and the beautiful. Since God is exalted above all that is knowable, only His bare existence is accessible to our intellect. In an attempt to blend Jewish and Hellenistic thought, Philo's aim essentially was to bring together and unify the two major categories of truth: human knowledge and divine revelation.

Ethical monotheism is not just a way of talking about God. It is a way of understanding human experience; it is a way of organizing the world in which we live. It is a faith that attempts to explain what we do not know by beginning with what we do know. We do know this world is rooted in a unity of our senses. We do know that defiance of moral law invites a disaster as devastating as any contempt for the laws of physics or chemistry or biology. We know, in short, that we cannot fathom it all and that this world is ultimately grounded in mystery. And that singular ethical mystery is what we call God.

THE PROBLEM OF EVIL

The most troublesome topic of all on the subject of God is the problem of evil. Almost from the beginning of time, philosophers and theologians have questioned how it could be possible for evil to thrive in a world created by one God who is good. No response has ever been wholly adequate. The mainstream of Jewish thought embraces a range of options, all of which deserve serious consideration and which may appeal to different individuals for reasons which only their own minds and hearts can know.

One explanation which may be found in certain philosophical systems, but seldom in Jewish sources, is essentially no explanation at all. It is a refusal to concede that evil exists. Advocates for this thesis contend that evil is simply an illusion, the absence of good. Goodness itself is the only certain reality; and wherever it does not yet exist, the resulting vacuum is a repository of what we call evil. If evil "exists" at all, it is only a category of thought that is equivalent to nonexistence.

A more widely held view in Judaism is a readiness to admit that evil does possess a reality of its own but that its nature transcends human understanding. It emphasizes, as we have already noted, that man's knowledge of God is limited, that his imperfect mind cannot possibly understand the divine purpose and therefore he must simply resign himself to only partial understanding. Since God's ways are not ours, it would be presumptuous for us to judge them. This is essentially the explanation for evil.

When the focus in Judaism shifts, however, to concerted efforts to explain evil in human terms, the resulting theories belong to one of several categories. The first category may be designated as moral explanations. Among these would be the thesis that evil is the result of wrong choices by individuals in their own personal lives. People are not puppets; if they are endowed by God with the freedom to choose between right and wrong, they must be prepared to accept the consequences of their actions. Freedom of choice is meaningless without the risk of error. That is the explicit lesson of the scriptural text which proclaims, "He who diligently seeks good seeks favor, but evil comes to him who searches for it. . . . He who troubles his household will inherit wind, and the fool will be servant to the wise" (Prov. 11:27, 29). Evil, in this view, is the consequence of poor judgment by individuals.

Another moral explanation rests upon a similar premise of poor judgment, except that the responsibility in this instance belongs to a group of people rather than to one alone. One person obviously cannot control the entire society in which he lives. His life is frequently conditioned by the decisions made by others, regardless of his own personal inclinations. Ignorance, poverty, persecution, and war are all evils perpetrated by whole governments, not single individuals. Nonetheless, even though he may not be personally accountable for all these wrongdoings, every individual pays for them as the price of living in concert with others. If one wishes to benefit from the advantages of a larger society, one must also be willing to suffer its shortcomings. The assets of living in society, however, far surpass its deficiencies. That unquestionably is what the Second Commandment emphasizes: "'For I the Lord your God am a jealous God, visiting the iniquity of the fathers upon the children to the third and the fourth generations of those who hate Me, but showing steadfast love to thousands of those who love Me and keep My commandments.'" (Exod. 20:4). It teaches that though God inflicts the sins of the parents upon the third and fourth generations of their children, He shows mercy to a thousand generations of those who revere Him and follow Him.

Still another moral explanation for the existence of evil, though not derived from any specific source in Jewish thought, is that it is a prerequisite for defining what is good. If evil were banished forever, the idea of goodness would be meaningless. People understand and appreciate what is right and just only in contrast to what is wrong and unjust. One is significant only as it helps to clarify and define its opposite. A world in which evil never occurs is also a world in which goodness is never noticed. Contrasting them is essential to knowing them.

Similarly, individuals could never be moral beings without the opportunity to choose between alternatives. As we observed in our statements about freedom of choice, a responsible decision can evolve only out of conscious deliberation between two moral options. A computer may be programmed for any eventuality; a person cannot be, without sacrificing his humanity. The existence of evil, then, ensures that he will remain a human creature, not a machine.

In addition to moral explanations for evil, Judaism also considers metaphysical theories. One such proposition is that evil is the result of viewing reality from a very narrow, limited range of vision or from an isolated stance. Natural disasters, in this context, may appear to be evil because of their devastating impact on people and property. At the same time, from a much larger perspective, they may contribute enormously to the ecological balance of nature and restore an environmental harmony indispensable to the earth and its inhabitants. In man's eye such events may be catastrophic; in God's eye they may well be supremely benevolent.

Similarly, a single act of nature can often be both a blessing and a curse. It all depends upon whom it affects. For a farmer, rain may be a welcome relief from a long drought. For a baseball player, it may result in a postponed game. Fire may burn and kill, but it can also heat and protect. How a person judges an act of nature depends upon his personal perspective and his needs.

Still another category of theories about the problem of evil might be termed futuristic, because they depend for verification upon the existence of a world other than our own. They originate primarily in an act of faith that cannot be verified by any empirical evidence, but only in the heart of the believer. Every attempt to explain the enigma of evil, of course, ultimately resides in an act of faith; but some, at least, begin by wrestling with observations about the world of experience.

A futuristic explanation, however, begins with certain articles of faith about a world beyond and proceeds to explain the world of immediate experience in terms of those beliefs. One such widespread theory in Judaism, as well as in other Western faiths, is anchored in the conviction that God rewards the righteous and punishes the wicked. Since it is clearly evident that life in this world does not always follow this pattern, advocates for this theory contend that ultimate justice is reserved for a life other than the one we know, an existence after death in which final rewards and punishments will rectify the injustices of this earthly existence. Experience in this world is not necessarily the final verdict on the merit of human conduct. The innocent who suffer in this life will prosper in another, just as the wicked who thrive in this world will eventually perish in the next.

Finally, one further effort to cope with evil in somewhat futuristic terms is one predicated on the premise that the world is incomplete. Evil is that portion of creation which has not yet been fully mastered and developed by man and God. It is the unfinished task of that divine and human partnership which exists to improve the quality of all life. It evolves out of the observation in Genesis that everything

God made he called "good," not "perfect." That distinction implies a continuing challenge and effort to join with God in eliminating evil by maximizing every potential for excellence which the world has possessed from the beginning. How well this world will perform depends upon how earnestly we struggle. Or, to explain the matter in terms of the Covenant, God counts on people, even as people count on God. Evil is the consequence of one disappointing the other.

A more recent variation of this explanation for evil flows from the aftermath of the Holocaust and the unbearable suffering which that unprecedented agony inflicted. Previously the view prevailed that if the people of Israel transgressed the Covenant, God would "hide His face" and permit the most grievous punishments to befall His people. If they failed in their observance, Israel could not escape the divine punishment for their faithlessness. Theoretically, God could insulate His people from terrible calamities if He chose; but He chose not to do so in view of their sinful deeds. Their punishment was perceived as a process of purification.

For many Jews in the post-Holocaust generation, that explanation has undergone a radical transformation. It was impossible for them to believe that God could have prevented such a catastrophe as the Holocaust but chose not to for whatever reasons, or that the Holocaust could have been punishment for human transgression of any sort.

Instead, they challenged the notion of Divine omnipotence on the grounds that God's gift of free will limited His own capacity to control human events. Evil then becomes the result of people deliberately abandoning God, not of God abandoning people. If people are endowed with free will, the world must be prepared to suffer the worst conceivable disasters that men may devise as well as the most valuable achievements they may produce. In a manner of speaking, God risked all possibilities in bestowing upon mankind the power to choose. The potential evil of such choice is the chance God takes as well as the chance man takes. In this view, the only way to destroy evil is to destroy free will, and that is a price neither God nor man would very likely be willing to pay.

Whatever explanation for evil seems most plausible, the emphasis in Judaism is always upon the urgency of coping with evil, not of speculating about it. It may be an impossible task to reconcile the existence of God with the existence of evil, but the world suffers from enough man-made misery and injustice to occupy the minds and hearts of concerned individuals for a lifetime. Much of what is wrong with the world is the result of human callousness and mismanagement. Judaism summons people to rectify those adversities within their reach, and the prescription for that undertaking is what it customarily terms the teaching of *Torah*.

The Torah is not only the grand design for achieving God's purpose in creation. It is also the instrument for achieving human fulfillment. Understanding Judaism is a matter of understanding the meaning and significance of Torah.

2
Torah: In Theory

The more Torah the more life, the more learning the more wisdom, the more counsel the more understanding, the more righteousness the more peace.

Hillel (30 B.C.E.–10 C.E.)

THE TORAH IN ITS LIMITED SCOPE

The basic sacred text of Judaism is not the "Old Testament." The proper word is simply the Bible, or the Hebrew Bible. The term "Old Testament" is appropriate only for those who believe that the Bible includes a "New Testament" and choose such a distinction to contrast the two major divisions of their sacred text. Since Judaism does not believe in a "New Testament," there is nothing "old" about its only Testament. That is why it is fitting to call it simply the Bible. That is the meaning of the term as it will be applied to this explanation of sacred Jewish texts.

The first section of the Hebrew Bible is the five books of Genesis through Deuteronomy whose authorship is attributed to Moses and called by the Hebrew name *Torah*. Those five books are also known in Hebrew as the *Chumash* ("the Five") and in Greek as the Pentateuch (stemming from Greek and Late Latin origins, referring to the first "five scrolls" or books of the Bible).

The second section of the Bible is designated as *N'vi-im,* which is the Hebrew term for "Prophets." This section includes all the literature attributed to those gifted individuals who were considered the recipients of privileged insights into the nature of God and his purpose.

All other books of the Bible constitute the third section which is understandably known as simply *K'tuvim,* "The Writings." This portion of the Bible contains some of the finest literature ever written, such as the Book of Psalms, Proverbs, Job, Song of Songs, both books of Samuel, Kings, and Chronicles.

All three sections of the Bible comprise a total of 39 books and are known collectively as *TaNaK*, which is an acronym derived from a combination of the first letters of each section in their Hebrew terminology (Torah, N'vi-im, and K'tuvim). *TaNaK* is the Hebrew word for Bible.

In its most limited sense, the term *Torah* stands for the Five Books of Moses: Genesis, Exodus, Leviticus, Numbers, and Deuteronomy. This section includes the story of creation and the Garden of Eden, the contributions of the Patriarchs, Abraham, Isaac, and Jacob, and their families, the enslavement of Israel in Egypt, and the Israelites' liberation from bondage under the leadership of Moses, the most favored of all the prophets. Moses brings Israel to the wilderness of Sinai for the revelation of the Ten Commandments and the entire body of teaching they are expected to follow in their observance of the Covenant.

The Torah contains numerous passages which remain forever central to Judaism, such as "You shall love your neighbor as yourself" (Lev. 19:18), and the words of the priestly benediction:

> "The Lord bless you and keep you:
> The Lord make His face to shine upon you,
> and be gracious to you:
> The Lord lift up His countenance upon you, and
> give you peace."
> [Num. 6:24–26]

The eternal Jewish affirmation of faith is also derived from the Torah with the injunction, known as the *Shema*:

> "Hear, O Israel: The Lord our God is one Lord; and you shall love the Lord your God with all your heart, with all your soul, and with all your might. And these words which I command you this day shall be upon your heart; you shall teach them diligently to your children, and shall talk of them when you sit in your house, and when you walk by the way, when you lie down, and when you rise up. And you shall bind them as a sign upon your hand, and they shall be as frontlets between your eyes. And you shall write them on the doorposts of your house and on your gates." [Deut. 6:4–9]

This crucial passage from Deuteronomy is taught to a Jewish child almost from the time he begins to speak. It is part of every Jewish worship service. Since worship is a daily religious exercise among many Jews, it is recited every day. Judaism teaches that it should also be the last words on the lips of every Jew who anticipates imminent death. Millions of martyrs marched to their death proclaiming the message of the Shema.

The teachings of the Torah are the most sacred legacy and inspiration of the Jewish people. They are so fundamental that they are recited in public reading every week of every year. The five books are divided into segments or portions, one of which is to be read on each successive Sabbath. Usually, the first words of each portion are chosen as the title, so that every week of the Jewish year can be identified by its Torah portion. In Hebrew, the segment is called a *sidrah* or *parshah*. The sidrah thus often provides a symbol for the week in which it occurs.

The Five Books of Moses are written in their original form on a parchment scroll by men called *Sofrim* (''scribes''), who have devoted their entire lives to copying the words of Scripture by hand, using special ink and goose quills for their task. A Jewish congregation may possess one or several scrolls, since no object in Jewish life is more precious than a Torah. All scrolls are placed in the *Aron Kodesh* (''holy ark'') in the synagogue and are removed only to be read, revered, or repaired.

Each Torah scroll contains exactly the same content. Each is a full text of Genesis through Deuteronomy. If a congregation is blessed with more than a single scroll, it may use one or more for special occasions and another for the weekly reading cycle on each Sabbath. A congregation with only one scroll must continually roll it from the weekly reading to special readings for various holidays and festivals.

Since the Torah is frequently called the ''crown of life,'' it is often decorated with a silver crown or a similar symbol of supreme authority. It is wrapped in a festive mantle and may also be embellished with a silver breastplate, the symbol of authority which presumably the High Priest wore in the ancient Temple in Jerusalem. Usually the accoutrements also include a *Yad* (''hand''), which is a silver ornament in the shape of a human finger and is used as a pointer for the leader to follow the reading in the text.

At a designated juncture in certain worship services, the holy ark is opened while the congregation rises. A scroll is removed from the ark and transported to the reading desk on the *Bimah* (''platform''). During the delivery of the Torah portion, the congregants are encouraged to follow in Hebrew-English Bibles provided for that purpose.

The sidrah is either read or chanted according to an ancient prescribed set of modes. The Torah text itself contains no vocalization signs, punctuation marks, or musical notations. The leader must know them all through previous preparation.

The parshah of the week is usually divided into sections of its own. This permits different members of the congregation to be called to the reading desk to offer blessings over the Torah before and after the reading of a particular section. Such an invitation is considered a significant honor and is customarily distributed to the most deserving congregants. Judaism teaches that actually every person is expected to prepare the weekly sidrah by examining the text prior to the service and searching every word for its meaning and significance. According to the tradition of Judaism, every word of the ancient text is sacred. Any scroll which contains an error is declared deficient or ''unkosher'' until the error is corrected. A Torah can never be deliberately destroyed. If it becomes too brittle or too fragile to use, it is buried in the earth just like a deceased person.

The other two major divisions of TaNaK are not read as frequently in the synagogue as the Torah. The weekly Torah reading, however, does include a selection from one of the two other major divisions of the Hebrew Bible and is referred to as the *haftarah* (''completion''). The haftarah may be a selection from the K'tuvim (''Writings'') or the N'viim (''Prophets''). Like the Torah portion, it is usually, though not always, chanted with its own distinctive melody. The haftarah designated for each sidrah usually focuses on a theme similar to that in the parshah or includes a reference to a significant individual or event mentioned in the Torah portion. From time to time, special occasions will dictate their own particular book of the TaNaK as the haftarah, such as the Book of Ruth on *Shavuoth*, or the Book of Jonah on the afternoon of *Yom Kippur.* Like the Torah portion, the haftarah is also preceded and followed by appropriate blessings.

The original sources for the teachings of the Torah are lost in antiquity. In all likelihood they were transmitted orally for countless generations before time and circumstances compressed them into written form. Reverence for these written words, however, probably developed at a very early date. Scholars who preserved the texts over the course of many centuries never even corrected obvious spelling errors in their manuscripts. They would simply add brief marginal explanations leaving the word intact but suggesting an alternate rendering for clearer definition. Out of veneration for what they considered to be divine revelation, they rejected every attempt to tamper with the text. Evidence of their success is more than ample, for if one compares the ancient manuscript fragments uncovered in archaeological excavations with the most recent printed editions, one discovers that, often with minor exceptions, one is almost a duplicate of the other. In more recent times, scholars have produced critical editions of the Torah and the TaNaK which seek to reconcile differences among various source materials. This process is called "lower biblical criticism."

More important than lower criticism is the field of higher criticism, which examines the veracity and reliability of the biblical subject matter itself. It rests upon a theory that the Bible is not the product of a single source but of several sources. The material which we possess as sacred literature in this view is actually a compilation of several authors whose work was eventually condensed and modified by a number of "editors" into its present form. Higher criticism also implied that many biblical events were committed to writing long after they actually occurred, which raised serious questions about their accuracy. Recent archaeological discoveries, however, clearly demonstrate that the biblical narrative is far more reliable for historical purposes than earlier skeptics had supposed.

THE TORAH IN ITS LARGER SCOPE

It is important to understand the word and concept of *Torah* in its broader context as well as in its narrower one. *Torah,* as a proper noun, refers specifically to the first five books of the TaNaK, the Five Books of Moses. The word *Torah,* however, can refer as a common noun to the entire domain of Jewish learning as a general discipline and supreme value. The sages enumerated a long list of urgent moral priorities for human conduct and concluded by stating, "And the study of Torah supersedes them all, because study is equal to them all." (*Kiddushin* 40B).

An understanding of this broader concept of Torah begins with a recognition that the word *Torah* does not mean "law." The word *Torah* derives from a Hebrew root which means literally "to teach" or "to guide." Torah, therefore, in its purest form is simply a term for "guidance" or "teaching." It is much more closely related to the notion of the Tao in Oriental thought, as the way or path to follow to total fulfillment, than it is to any Western concept of law. Torah is the necessary ingredient in the message of Proverbs that enables a person to "train up a child in the way he should go, and when he is old he will not depart from it" (Prov. 22:6).

In this respect, Torah did not cease with the death of Moses or the books attributed to him. The prophets continued the process; their successors included the poets and sages who contributed books like Psalms, Proverbs, Ecclesiastes, and Job. Even though these books were not part of the original Torah, they certainly followed in the spirit of Torah.

That same spirit continued in the teachings of the rabbinic sages, which span a period of nearly eight hundred years from the third century before the Common Era to the fifth century of the Common Era. Their work began with the *Mishnah* and culminated in the *Talmud*, which will be discussed further on. These compilations, however, all reflected the expansion of Torah by consolidating, amplifying, and clarifying the inherited teachings of earlier generations.

Both the Bible and rabbinic literature eventually inspired an abundance of informed commentaries and interpretations. All of them added still further to the wealth of insight and learning that necessarily preceded a life of fulfillment and purpose. An appreciation for Torah inevitably includes an awareness of the moralists and philosophers who throughout Jewish history expanded the horizons of Jewish learning and living.

Torah thus begins in the Pentateuch, but it does not end there. It really has no end, because Torah is a constant, timeless quest for maximizing the spiritual potential of the human soul. That is a task which can never be complete. Every effort to stretch the mind and heart to their farthest reaches is an effort of Torah. Torah, in its broadest context, is the repository of all Jewish learning from the earliest of times to our own.

The terms of the Covenant between God and Israel reflect this diversity of the term *Torah*. The Covenant is first a derivative of the legacy called the Written Torah. The Written Torah is that document which, so far as we can determine, was initially proclaimed to the people of Israel in relatively complete form by Ezra the Scribe in 444 B.C.E. The account of that presentation can be found in Nehemiah 9 and 10.

This Written Torah presumed that the society which it governed was predominantly agrarian. It was and is a blueprint of religious observance for people closely tied to the land. Holidays are largely harvest festivals and feast days, at least in their origins. The ritual system caters to the needs and requirements of a farming community. Repentance and atonement are defined in terms of an elaborate sacrificial cult in which transgressors may seek divine forgiveness by parting with the best portion of their crops or the finest of their flocks and herds. Even rewards and punishments are worded in agricultural terms. If people observe the commandments, God will bless them with adequate rain, abundant harvests, and healthy livestock. If they violate those commandments, the land will fail them; and they will be cursed by drought, mildew, pestilence, and famine.

The organizational structure inherent in the Written Torah was also deeply rooted in the soil. The principal religious authority was a priestly class which administered the Written Torah and presided over the sacrificial cult which was centered in the major religious institution, the Temple in Jerusalem. The general community was required to support the priesthood by tithing (contributing one tenth) of the fruits of their labor as part of their religious obligation.

The mechanism for the ceremonial service to God was the sacrificial cult. Only what the land produces and provides was suitable fare for such sacrifice.

Although biblical scholars generally agree that in earliest times several sites were certified for authentic religious observance, eventually the Temple in Jerusalem became the only permissible place to worship God with the apparatus of a sacrificial system. These were all provisions of the Written Torah.

In addition to the Written Torah, a verbal tradition which complemented, clarified, and expanded the Written Torah achieved prominence some time during the Second Commonwealth. This tradition was known as the Oral Law in contrast to the Written Law of the Torah. The Oral Law was a compilation of teachings whose origins probably derived from the dawn of Jewish history and which had been expounded and expanded by each succeeding generation. Traditional Judaism teaches that the contributions of all these generations were revealed to Moses at Mt. Sinai, together with the Written Law; therefore, they are invested with the same supreme significance as the Torah itself. Again, in the traditional view, the Written Law and Oral Law are inseparable, because both encompass the totality of divine teaching which contains all knowledge for all time to come.

A more historical view of the Oral Law attributes its origins to the limitations of the Written Law in the Torah. This view does not deny the antiquity of these oral teachings by successive generations, but contends that they were basically an attempt, through interpretation and amplification, to adapt the Torah to changing times and circumstances. As an agrarian society acquired a more urban character, as a diversity of trades and crafts developed, as the world expanded geographically, it became increasingly urgent to deepen and broaden the application of the Written Law to ensure its relevance and vitality. That was the function of the Oral Law.

In many ways, the Oral Law served a purpose for the Written Law which was not much different from that which the opinions of the Supreme Court serve for the Constitution of the United States. Even though the principles remain firm, the conditions which originally inspired the Constitution have changed considerably. It would be exceedingly difficult, if not impossible, to apply the Constitution as it was initially designed in 1789 to America at the threshold of the twenty-first century. What enables our own nation to retain its flexibility is the body of constitutional law that evolved from the deliberations of the Supreme Court about the Constitution. In Judaism, deliberations about the Torah evolved into the Oral Law.

In the second century, Rabbi Judah the Prince recognized that the rapidly increasing body of tradition could no longer be preserved and perpetuated orally, even in times of relative peace and tranquility. It was difficult to find scholars who could absorb the enormous quantity of information that had accumulated for several centuries. Rabbi Judah therefore decided to edit in written form the oral traditions of the past.

The Oral Torah was organized into six sections or "orders." This first codification of Jewish teaching following the Torah, done in the second century, was called the *Mishnah* ("Repetition"). Its legal decisions were based upon, though not limited to, the Written Law and developed out of intensive discussions and debates among leading scholars. All opinions about the interpretation of Scripture, however, were subject to the test of certain rules or "hermeneutic" explanatory principles that had been formulated by the rabbinic sage Hillel.

The Mishnah is a remarkable repository of criticism and dissent which clearly verifies the extraordinary range of intellectual freedom which Judaism permitted and encouraged. Few if any ancient religious traditions ever enshrined for posterity, as Judaism did, the minority view as well as the majority. In the language of the Mishnah itself, "This side and that one are both the words of the living God." Elsewhere, the sages observed that no one could ever be certain whether the minority view of an earlier generation might not become the majority view of a later one, and vice versa.

The regulations which governed the daily routines of Jewish life and determined the pattern of conduct for all occasions in all places were catalogued under a general rubric called *Halakah*, which is perhaps best translated as "the way" of acceptable Jewish conduct. In addition to Halakah, the system also included a body of instruction which explained, expanded, and often embellished the law under consideration by clarifying its principal or larger significance. Such material often followed the pattern of teaching by maxim, legend, or parable, or by a homiletical treatment of the text. This segment of the literature was known as *Aggadah*, which means literally "the telling" of the story, or in modern terminology, preaching.

The Aggadah may not only be found as an integral part of the Mishnah, but also as a separate literary enterprise attached to the text of Scripture itself and arranged as a commentary. In this independent form, the material is classified as *Midrash*, which means "the search" with reference to new or hidden meanings in the Written Law.

Halakah and Aggadah interact very closely. They are exceedingly difficult to separate. One reinforces the other and complements the other. Halakah addresses the question of what a Jew should do while Aggadah explains why he should do it.

After the codification of the Mishnah, the same process which had necessitated an expansion of the Written Law now also necessitated an expansion of the Mishnah. Beginning with the rabbinic sages Rav and Shmuel in the third century, the leading scholars examined closely the text of the Mishnah they had inherited and eventually developed a formidable collection of their own interpretations and modifications based on their careful review and scrutiny of the Mishnaic text. The lengthy discussions and decisions they rendered were also committed to writing and were called collectively the *Gemara*, signifying the "completion" of the Mishnah. The Gemara could always be distinguished linguistically as well as conceptually from the Mishnah by reference to the titles assigned to the teachers of each source. The teachers of the Mishnah were known as the *Tannaim* ("teachers"). Those responsible for the Gemara were known to posterity as the *Amoraim* ("interpreters").

The fusion of the Mishnah with the Gemara, the combined teachings of the Tannaim and the Amoraim, produced the voluminous, supreme classical postbiblical work of Jewish antiquity, the *Talmud*. The Talmud is an exceedingly difficult library of books on virtually every conceivable subject of human concern. To be fully understood, it cannot be read casually; it must be studied carefully. Even the serious student would find it almost unintelligible without the contribution of brilliant medieval commentators, the most famous of whom was Rabbi Solomon ben Isaac, better known as Rashi. Rashi and others wrote running commentaries to almost every sentence and word of the text. Their explanations were found along the margins of every page of the Talmud.

The text of the Talmud reflects consistently a firm belief in the absolute truth of the Torah, the Written Law. For the rabbinic mind, the truths of the Torah were perfect and immutable. If any statement in the Torah seemed superfluous, contradictory, or obsolete, the problem derived not from the text but from the inadequate understanding of the reader. Indeed, apparent difficulties in the text were often cited as clues or hints to exceptionally profound and mysterious meanings.

If one interpretation did not fit the requirements of the Torah, the only recourse was to change the interpretation, not the Torah. This supreme trust in the process of interpretation may seem contrived to the modern mind, but it was essentially an effort to maintain the continuity of Judaism without tarnishing the integrity of the Torah.

The world of the sixth century, when the Talmud was finally codified, was radically different from the biblical age of the Torah. In addition to a drastic transformation in the realm of ideas and observance, the institutional apparatus which determined the organizational structure of the Jewish community had completely changed. In place of the Temple, which had been destroyed in the first century, the principal religious institution was now the synagogue. As a consequence, the prevailing authority in Jewish life was no longer the hereditary priest who supervised the service of the Temple, but the rabbi who taught in the synagogue and whose authority rested on criteria of scholarship and learning to which any student might aspire, regardless of birth. With the destruction of the Temple, the sacrificial cult also ceased to function as the mechanism for divine service to God. Worship with words replaced offerings of various kinds. Instead of sacrifice supervised by the priesthood, collections of prayer sanctioned by the rabbis ensured communication with God. A system of sacrifice directed by a priesthood in a single Temple structure had yielded to a system that centered in a multiplicity of synagogues led by rabbis in which the primary form of worship was verbal prayer.

One system did not relinquish its authority to the other gracefully. The transition was a bitterly contested battle with ardent defenders on each side seeking to consolidate their own claims to authority. The supporters of the Written Law and its institutions were known primarily as Sadducees; most were temple priests and their families. They denied the validity of the oral tradition and regarded only the written text as a legitimate authority. They interpreted its teachings in very strict and literal terms.

The staunch supporters of the Oral Law were essentially the rabbinic teachers who came to be known as the Pharisees. The Pharisees were a Jewish religious and political party or sect during the Second Temple period which emerged as a distinct group shortly after the Hasmonean Revolt, about 165–160 B.C.E. Many scholars agree they were probably the successors of the *Hasidim*, an earlier Jewish sect which promoted the observance of Jewish ritual and the study of Torah. The Pharisees considered themselves the traditional followers of Ezra the Scribe, whom they cherished after Moses as the founder of Judaism. In upholding a reverence for the Oral Law, they tried to adapt old codes to new conditions and emphasized the beliefs in a combination of free will and predestination, in the resurrection of the dead and rewards for this life in a world to come.

At first the Pharisees were relatively few in number; but by the first century C.E., they became the spokesmen for the religious beliefs, practices, and social attitudes of the vast majority of the Jewish people. They attempted to imbue the masses with a spirit of holiness by scrupulous observance of the Torah and by spreading traditional religious teachings. In contrast to more radical groups, the Pharisees were even willing to submit to foreign domination, so long as it did not interfere with their inner life, rather than support an impious government of their own.

No group in history has ever suffered a worse distortion of its character than have the Pharisees through parts of the Gospels in the New Testament. Taking its cue from Christian Scriptures, Western tradition has associated the term *Pharisee* with a person satisfied simply with the mere externals of religion, or else a hypocrite. The Pharisees themselves acknowledged the danger of limiting Judaism to the mechanical performance of rituals; yet the denunciations in the New Testament are not confined to potential aberrations, but to all of Pharisaism and to all the Pharisees. Earlier generations of Christian scholars endorsed those denunciations and tended to label all of Judaism as no more than the hollow shell of religious observance or as pure and simple hypocrisy. The historical record will not support those conclusions.

Beginning about the second century, the Pharisaic teachers all carried the title of *rabbi*. In order to find support in the Torah for their oral traditions and thereby discredit the claims of the Sadducees, the rabbis devised an explanatory method of Midrash as an instrument of interpretation. Midrash may be viewed as a profound and mystical treatment of sacred literature. It may also be seen as a free, creative, and occasionally contrived method of extracting meaning from the text, one that served the Pharisees exceedingly well in adapting the content of revelation to meet their needs and purposes in their clash with the Sadducees. Midrash is also a resourceful mechanism for adapting and rendering more flexible the rigid presumptions of the scriptural text.

Most Jews eventually identified the meaning of the Written Law with the teachings of the Oral Law as the rabbis explained them. The development of Judaism to the present day was largely the achievement of the Pharisees. Thus, the commandment of ''eye for eye, tooth for tooth'' (Exod. 21:24) was not taken literally, but understood as meaning that one who injures another must compensate his victim fairly. ''You shall not boil a kid in its mother's milk'' (Exod. 23:19) was extended to include a prohibition against mixing any kind of meat with milk or milk products.

In the eighth century, there emerged a counter trend which temporarily challenged the supremacy of the Oral Law and rabbinic Pharisaic Judaism. The adversaries of Talmudic interpretation were called *Karaites* (''Scripturalists''). They championed a return to the position of the Sadducees and a decision to live strictly by the simple word of the Written Law. The proposal was far easier to advocate than to execute. The Karaites disagreed even among themselves about the true meaning of the commandments. The central issue still remained a need for flexibility to ensure the continued growth and vitality of Jewish life. When the Karaites failed to absorb that message, they sealed their own eventual demise.

The terms of the Covenant evolved, therefore, out of the text of the Written Torah, interpreted by the teachings of the Oral Law as it was developed by the Pharisees. That combination comprises the main body of Jewish tradition and includes several distinctive ideas and values which merit thoughtful consideration for an adequate understanding of Judaism and its Covenant.

SOME IDEALS OF TORAH

At the very heart of the Covenant is a supreme emphasis on the importance of learning and study. The Mishnah teaches that ''he who does not learn forfeits his life'' (*Avot* 1:13). The Talmud further records a discussion in which the question was raised, ''Which is more important, study or good deeds?'' Rabbi Tarphon replied that good deeds were more important, but Rabbi Akiba insisted that study was greater. Eventually, they both agreed that study was greater, because study leads to the performance of good deeds. They also declared that one who does not have a knowledge of Torah and Mishnah cannot be considered a cultured person (*Kiddushin* 40b).

Rabbinic literature exhibits an abundance of evidence for the priority of learning in Jewish life. The sages taught that "he who does not increase his knowledge decreases it" (*Avot* 1:13). Elsewhere they asked, "Who are the guardians of the community?" and replied, "The scribes and teachers" (*Jerushalmi: Chagiga* 2). One of the most instructive passages on this subject is the Talmudic explanation of the biblical verse from 1 Chronicles 16:22 in which the rabbis declare that "'Touch not my anointed ones' refers to school children, and 'do my prophets no harm' refers to disciples of the Sages" (*Shabbat* 119b).

In Talmudic and medieval times, boys began their schooling at the age of five; girls were not bound by any requirements for formal education, but they learned to read and write at home. School routines were difficult, and the hours were exceedingly long, sometimes continuing long after dark. The Talmud stipulated that every father was obliged to teach his son an honorable trade. In the ghettos of the Middle Ages, however, vocational training of any kind was a fantasy for most Jews; the labor guilds that controlled the work force ensured that most trades and skilled crafts were closed to any Jew. The study and teaching of Talmud evolved into a fulltime occupation.

The absence of ordinary vocational opportunities for Jews may have contributed paradoxically to the emphasis on learning in Judaism, which persisted even in its most oppressed periods. The leaders of the Jewish community were not men of political or military power. Authority was therefore delegated to religious spokesmen who were the only acknowledged leaders among the people. The rabbis and scholars formulated the laws that governed their followers. The highest prestige and status in the Jewish world therefore centered in the rabbinate. The rabbi was the most venerated and respected individual in a young boy's life. He might never be able to emulate a count, a duke, or a prince; but he could aspire to become a rabbi. When it became evident that success required study, learning was invested with supreme value.

Learning was supreme for an even more basic reason. Fulfilling the Covenant with God required a Jew to observe its terms. He could not observe its terms without understanding them. Understanding required study. Study was consequently the key to spiritual fulfillment. The study of the Torah was "a tree of life to those who lay hold [to it]" (Prov. 3:18).

Judaism, as we have already noted, teaches that learning for its own sake is an exercise in futility. Only study that leads to action deserves serious consideration. Action and human conduct are the basic criteria of reverence for God. What a person believes is a reflection of what he does, not what he says.

The Covenant is almost entirely a prescription for right action and right conduct. A proper treatment of its terms requires first an explanation of its suppositions about human nature on which all moral judgments depend.

Judaism contends that a person is neither basically good nor basically evil. Every individual is born with two conflicting inclinations. One is the *yetzer hatov,* the passive or positive impulse; the other is the *yetzer hara,* the active or aggressive impulse. The yetzer hatov is the innate drive for all creative and constructive action—music, poetry, art, as well as moral concern for justice, love, compassion, righteousness. The yetzer hara is by contrast the innate drive for personal aggrandizement—the competitive instinct, greed, envy, lust, and the temptation to succeed at any cost. This aggressive impulse, however, is not entirely negative or destructive. According to a Midrash, it may even be channeled into positive directions, "For were it not for the aggressive impulse, no man would build a house, nor marry a wife, nor beget children, nor engage in a trade" (*Kohelet Rabbah* 3:11). Elsewhere in the Midrash, the aggressive impulse is reduced almost to a neutral force which a person may then manipulate for good or evil purposes. A constructive application of that impulse will derive from observance of the Torah, as the Midrash explains: "Like iron, out of which man can fashion whatever implements he pleases when he heats it in the forge, so the aggressive impulse can be subdued to the service of God if tempered by the word of the Torah which is like fire" (*Avot de-Rabbi Natan, Perek* 16).

With this set of premises about the nature of the human condition, the rabbinic sages concluded that sin or wrongdoing was a state of action, not a state of being. They taught that Adam's disobedience in the Garden of Eden was not an Original Sin which contaminated all future generations of mankind, but that it was a prototype of the kind of transgression to which all people may succumb as a result of their own inadequacies. The "fall" of Adam is an object lesson in the inevitable limitations of finite creatures. The rabbis carefully emphasized the full responsibility of every individual for his or her own sin despite the effects of Adam's "fall."

Nowhere in its literature does Judaism summon a person to atone for some burden of guilt inherited from the past. No sacrifices in the ancient Temple at Jerusalem were ever associated with such an eternal transgression. No ceremonies or rituals even hinted at such a concept. Judaism also never embraced the hope that God would in some manner intervene in the affairs of a doomed humanity to remove the curse of this guilt from Adam's descendants and to redeem people from their corrupt, evil nature.

In Jewish tradition, the sin of Adam did not extinguish man's moral freedom or initiative. The major concentration has always been directed not to the origin of sin, but to the avoidance of wrongdoing and to the adoption of ways to eliminate it. No person is condemned to sin; but all people are capable of it, simply because all people are endowed with free will.

Jewish theology teaches that if a person has committed a sin, he or she may repent and be forgiven. The initiative, however, must come from the person, not from God. The Psalmist declared that "the Lord is near to all who call upon Him in truth" (Ps. 145:18). The prophet Malachi assured his listeners, "Return to Me, and I will return to you, says the Lord of hosts" (Mal. 3:7). In every instance, however, the effort begins with man.

In Judaism, the highest of virtues is repentance. No other religious literature is more eloquent on the subject. The Talmud teaches that "in the place where a repentant sinner stands, even the righteous who have never sinned cannot stand" (*Berachot* 34b). Furthermore, repentance in Judaism is not a mystery or a sacrament. It does not imply any miraculous transformations in the individual or the rebirth of his soul. Rather, repentance is largely a human undertaking. It involves a four-step process that begins with a readiness to acknowledge a wrongdoing, followed by acts of compensation for the injury inflicted, and genuine resolve to avoid a repetition of the same sinful deed. Only then can a person continue with the fourth and final step of praying for forgiveness and cherish the expectation of receiving God's mercy.

In Jewish tradition, life is entirely a matter of choices. One may choose either good or evil. From the moment of birth, every person is a free agent. One may sin, or one may avoid it. One surely is not perfect, but every person is certainly perfectible; and one's purpose in life is to achieve as much of that moral potential as one's humanity will allow. The task is not to eliminate aggressive inclinations, but to control them. A person can be all that God meant him or her to be, or that person may ignore the opportunity. All depends on individual choice.

Judaism has always emphasized that people please God most by their deeds. It is deeds which make atonement for man. It is deeds which demonstrate his spiritual growth and maturity. The Psalmist declared that God judges man according to his deeds (Ps. 7:9). The Midrash claims that "one cannot obtain rewards except for deeds" (*Mechiltah* I, 34). Faith is important, but performance is primary.

One of the Hebrew terms for faith is *emunah*. Emunah derives from the same linguistic root as *aman*, which means "craftsman" or "master workman." Emunah, or faith, in Judaism is a way, a skillful technique for fulfilling the moral purpose in creation. Faith is wholehearted concentration in the service of God, both in word and in deed.

Jews believe, as part of their observance of the Covenant, that they are summoned by God to dream, to strive, and to build—again and again—upon the ruins of all their shattered hopes and ideals. That is the true test of human integrity, and that is a principal insight which flows from the wisdom of a people who have known many sorrows and many disasters. It flows from the experience of a people too optimistic to be impatient, and too old to be cynical. Believing Jews will risk any possibilities, because all of them will include the presence of God.

One of the inevitable possibilities is always death. In Judaism, death was perceived as retribution for sin. In relating the story of Genesis, the rabbis noted that had Adam not sinned by tasting of the fruit of the tree of knowledge, he would never have died. Adam was created without the inevitable prospect of dying. He brought upon himself the end of his life through his own transgression.

The High Holy Day liturgy in Judaism graphically portrays this thought. We are urged to choose life and not death, by choosing good and not evil. Evil is associated with death; good is synonymous with life. If one does evil, one dies. If one does good, one lives.

Closely allied to this concept of death is the idea of resurrection. *T'chiat hametim*, or "resurrection of the dead," is a fundamental rabbinic concept, almost a doctrine in fact. The rabbis insisted on few matters of belief, but resurrection was one of them. Those who renounced it had no share in "the world to come." The rabbis were not abstract thinkers or philosophers. They thought and taught in concrete terms. If there was to be immortality and a Final Judgment, people had to retain their particular physical distinctions. Not even God could judge a disembodied spirit. At the end of time, therefore, God would recreate from the dust of the earth a new body for every soul identical in appearance to its earthly form.

The progression of time in rabbinic thought was divided into three epochs. *Olam hazeh*, or "this world," was the universe we presently inhabit. The events of the past and present all occur in this world. We live in it; we think in it; and we shall die in it.

What follows this world in the order of time are *y'mot hamashiach*, or "the days of the Messiah." At this point biblical sources divulge two threads of Jewish thought about the coming of the Messianic Age. The first concept of the Messiah which derives from prophetic literature may be termed the "horizontal view." In this context the Messiah and the Messianic Age will arrive as the consequence of a normal progression in human history, a state of affairs which will come about not as the result of any miracles or divine intervention, but as a product of the normal course of human events, the interaction of human effort and conduct. This view presumes that the history of mankind is purposeful. People by their own initiative and determination may hasten the fulfillment of all their noblest goals and aspirations. This is the vision of the future that:

> It shall come to pass in the latter days
> that the mountain of the house of the Lord
> shall be established as the highest of the mountains,
> and shall be raised above the hills;

and all the nations shall flow to it,
and many peoples shall come and say:
"Come, let us go up to the
mountain of the Lord,
to the house of the God of Jacob;
that He may teach us His ways
and that we may walk in His paths."
For out of Zion shall go forth the law,
and the word of the Lord from Jerusalem.
[Isa. 2:2–3]

By contrast, the last chapters of the Book of Daniel present an entirely different notion of messianism. There the Messiah, or "deliverer," is the product not of ordinary history, of straight-line or horizontal development. He is the product of God's direct intervention. This is a "vertical" view of Messianic hope. God bursts onto the stage of human history and sends His messenger to redeem a world which man has entirely mismanaged and betrayed. The Messianic Age is a vertical action on God's part, breaking unexpectedly into history and saving His universe.

Regardless of the distinctions, both concepts of the Messianic Age shared the conclusion that the y'mot hamashiach would succeed this world, the olam hazeh. During the Messianic Age people would live in peace and harmony with each other, all fear and anxiety would vanish, and virtue would reign supreme. The Messianic Age would be a direct extension of the present world of time and place. It would ensure the complete fulfillment of the hopes and aspirations of people everywhere.

The third division of time in rabbinic thought, or the sequel to the Messianic Age, was the *olam haba*, or the "world to come." This distant reality was an existence not of this world. This was the afterlife, the immortal state of the human soul, an existence subject not to human time, but to God's time. This was eternity. The olam haba would be ushered in by God Himself. This would be the occasion for the resurrection of all the dead, for the Final Judgment, and for the reparation of injustice.

The Midrash reports that on one occasion Rabbi Yochanan said, "Not like the Jerusalem of this world is the Jerusalem of the 'world to come.' The Jerusalem of this world: All who wish to ascend to it may ascend. That of the world to come: There they only will enter who are called'' (*Baba Batra* 75b). The olam haba is actually the end of time, the beginning of eternity when the righteous will bask in the radiance of divine light, and the wicked will be consigned to the darkness of eternal oblivion. So did the ancient traditions hold, and so do they still among most Jews.

3

Torah: In Practice

Religion embraces both faith and action. The primary quality is action, for it lays the foundation for faith: the more we do good, the more readily do we grasp the meaning of duty and life and the more readily do we believe in the divine from which stems the good.

Leo Baeck (1873–1956)

THE MEANING OF MITZVAH

These teachings about the perception of reality and the universe explain not just the unparalleled greatness of the rabbinic notions of life, the Messiah, and the world to come. They enable us especially to understand the supreme consequence of the ethics of Judaism. The rabbinic attitudes toward death, resurrection and the Messianic Age define for Judaism the meaning of human responsibility. The task of man is to join with God in the redemption of this world, and not to prepare one's self for a life after death.

The rabbis urged right conduct not for the sake of reward, but for its own sake. The Messianic Age was not so much a promise of reward as it was an inevitable outcome of right relationships between human beings. The world, the rabbis noted, was not created perfect. God said only that it was good. Only man can improve on what God has already made. This is at once his distinction and his obligation. The sages tell us that when God created the first man, He showed him all the trees of the Garden of Eden and said to him, "'See My works, how fine and excellent they are. Now all that I have created, I have created for you. Think upon this and do not corrupt and desolate My world; for if you corrupt it, there is no one to set it right after you'" (*Ecclesiastes Rabbah* VII, 28).

For Judaism, the future of the world, its perfection, and beauty, depend upon man. How much more appropriate could such a theme possibly be in an age that pursues power at the risk of its own self-destruction?

Planning, striving, and living for the world that God intended is what Judaism implies by the term *salvation*. Salvation is not an individual experience, because the task is too demanding for any solitary person. Salvation is necessarily a collective undertaking. It is that concentrated effort in search of the Messianic Age when people will be at one with themselves, with their neighbors and with God. That is the world of redemption. And since man is slowly approaching this blissful existence continually, one may speak in Judaism of God redeeming the world every day. Every day the quest is closer to fulfillment. In rabbinic thinking man needs not to be saved from evil; he needs to be saved for a better world.

Judaism radiates a fundamental optimism about the nature of man. Man can, if he will, transform his world into paradise. The agonies and crises which afflict the human condition can be faced and defeated with sufficient will and determination. The Midrash states that:

> Rabbi Joshua ben Levi once came upon Elijah standing at the entrance to the cave of Rabbi Simeon ben Yochai. He said to Elijah: "When will the Messiah come?"
>
> He said: "Go ask him."
>
> —And where is he to be found?
>
> —At the gates of Rome . . .
>
> Rabbi Joshua went there. He said to the Messiah: "Peace to you, my master and teacher . . ."
>
> He said: "When will the master come?"
>
> He said: "Today."
>
> —Rabbi Joshua went back to Elijah and said to him: "He confused me, for he said he would come today; and he has not come."
>
> Elijah said to him: "Thus he said to you: Today—if you would but listen to His voice" (*Sanhedrin* 98a).

The Midrash emphasized that the Messiah will come only when human beings repent and begin together the practice of righteous deeds. The remaining distance is still enormous, but so is the untapped potential in human nature.

That untapped potential requires careful guidance and direction. The instrument of such guidance is the Torah and the Covenant.

The primary purpose of the Torah is to teach mankind to obey God's moral law. That moral law is largely a network of principles that govern the way people treat each other. Those principles in Hebrew are called *mitzvot,* the singular form being *mitzvah.*

The meaning of mitzvah is difficult to understand, for the word is no less difficult to translate. It has been defined as "commandment," "commitment," "responsibility," or "obligation." Any single word is unlikely to convey the unique meaning of mitzvah with all its overtones. Mitzvah is probably best understood as "a deliberate act which enables a person to approximate divine activity." It is a way to holiness.

Mitzvah is the word Judaism invokes to describe an act of ethical distinction. Any act of kindness or support for a deserving cause, for example, is called a mitzvah. The Talmud teaches that it is even a mitzvah to keep one's body clean, to reconcile those who quarrel, to feed animals before one's self, to visit the sick, to bury the dead, and to comfort the mourners. Whatever dignifies life or enhances life is a mitzvah.

The performance of mitzvot is the basis for righteous conduct between one person and all others. Whatever spark of divinity one person possesses, all people possess. It cannot be withheld or withdrawn from anyone. It exists equally in people of all races, colors, creeds, and faiths. Economic class or social status are irrelevant in assessing the divine endowment of every human person. If there is one God, there can be only one humanity.

If God created man in His own image, no individual can exaggerate his respect for another. To the contrary, since every person is endowed with divine attributes, his moral worth is infinite.

In its practical application, the performance of mitzvot forbids the use of any individual as an instrument in the service of any other. One is not permitted to injure another in any manner, or to oppress, exploit, or humiliate him. Consequently, one may not deceive a person or even withhold the truth from him, since, as the sages explained, words may cut and kill just as savagely as any sword of steel.

Righteous living in terms of mitzvah is more than just a matter of abstaining from evil. It requires active protest and performance in defiance of evil. The rabbis taught that:

> Whoever can protest and prevent his household from committing a sin and does not, is accountable for the sins of his household; if he could protest and prevent his fellow-citizens (and does not), he is accountable for the sins of his fellow citizens; if the whole world, he is accountable for the whole world. [*Shabbat* 54b]

One of the axioms of rabbinic ethics is that a society which does not allow protest is doomed. One source (*Seder Eliahu Rabbah* 8) contends that the Egyptians drowned in the Red Sea, because they blindly followed Pharaoh's unjust decrees, while another (*Shabbat* 199b) concludes that Jerusalem fell to the Romans, because her people failed to rebuke each other.

The performance of ethical mitzvot, however, does not demand inordinate courage or excessive heroics. Righteous conduct is much more a matter of the constant, continuous practice of good deeds. It is a timeless prescription for a healthy society. One such principle is *tzedakah*. This Hebrew term is best defined not as "charity," but, in faithfulness to its authentic root, as "justice" or "righteousness."

Giving to those in need or to urgent causes is not, for Judaism, simply a matter of love or compassion. Tzedakah is an obligation required by law as something that is right, not just kind or thoughtful. As early as the time of the Mishnah, Jewish communities organized systems of progressive taxation to meet the needs of their indigent neighbors. The Mishnah instructs every person to leave unharvested at least a sixtieth of his field; how far one's obligation might exceed the minimum depended on the size of the field and the extent of poverty among the people.

The highest form of tzedakah was a concerted effort to restore to the poor the dignity of their own independence. Moses Maimonides, the foremost medieval Jewish authority, declared that:

> [The highest level of charity] is to anticipate charity by preventing poverty; namely, to assist the reduced fellow man, either by a considerable gift or a loan of money, or by teaching him a trade, or by putting him in the way of business, so that he may earn an honest livelihood, and not be forced to the dreadful alternative of holding out his hand for charity. [*Yad ha-Hazakah, H. Tzedakah* 10, as translated in *Union Prayerbook* 2 (Cincinnati: Central Conference of American Rabbis, 1949), p. 118.]

Even as the donor was expected to contribute his best, so, too, was the recipient subject to the same obligation. Moral integrity in Judaism required a poor person to accept any kind of job, however menial, in preference to any charitable gift. According to Talmudic law, the community was not required to support one who was able but refused to work. In the Middle Ages, justice yielded to compassion and pity in gradually evolving the legendary figure of the professional *schnorrer*, a kind of lovable beggar.

Whatever the mitzvah of moral obligation might entail, the property rights of any individual never superseded basic human needs. Jewish law endorsed the principle of private ownership and guarded the rights of an individual to manage his own property. Nonetheless, ownership was ultimately construed in terms of stewardship. Wherever people lived, they were basically tenants subject to God, Who was literally the land Lord.

Since all property essentially belongs to God, it may not be manipulated for immoral purposes, such as exploiting or ignoring the rightful needs of others. The Talmud stipulates that if two people are living in a house which begins sinking into the ground, the person on the upper level is obligated to join with the individual on the lower level in finding a new dwelling for him when his unit becomes untenable (*Baba Batra* 6b–7a).

The precept of tzedakah is not much less a priority among ethical mitzvot than the emphasis on the pursuit of peace. Peace or *shalom* is the highest and most urgent of all moral imperatives. The Mishnah attributes to Hillel the summons, "Be of the disciples of Aaron, one who loves peace and pursues it, who loves all men and brings them near to the Torah" (*Avot* 1:12). The Midrash further explains: "The Law does not order you to run after, or pursue the [other] commandments, but only to fulfill them when the appropriate occasion arises. . . . But peace you must seek in your own place and run after it to another" (*Numbers Rabbah, Hukkat*).

Elsewhere the Talmud declares: "It is proper to help the Gentile poor as well as the poor of Israel. It is proper to visit the Gentile sick as well as the sick of Israel. It is proper to bury the bodies of Gentiles as well as the bodies of Israelites. These acts are proper, because they promote peace" (*Gittin,* 61a).

Peace is so imperative that a person is even permitted to lie or suffer humiliation in order to preserve it. One of the most eloquent illustrations of this precept is the famous incident recorded in the Midrash about the married couple who were quarreling because the woman spent so much time listening to the words of Rabbi Meir.

Finally, the husband expelled his wife from their home and told her not to come back until she had spit in the eye of her famous teacher. The woman, of course, was appalled at even the thought of such a deed; but Rabbi Meir learned of her husband's directive and formulated a solution. The next time the woman attended his lecture, he complained of an ailment in his eye which only she could relieve by spitting in his eye seven times. Reluctant as she was to oblige, the woman finally consented after Rabbi Meir demanded her cooperation.

After the woman left, the students objected to the course of action Rabbi Meir had chosen, arguing that such lying and humiliation had disgraced both their teacher and the Torah. They would have recommended physical punishment for the husband until he agreed to respect his wife.

Rabbi Meir replied by citing a lesson of Rabbi Ishmael who proclaimed: "So great is peace that God has permitted people even to blot out His Holy Name in water in order to achieve it."

"Therefore," said Rabbi Meir, "if the Holy Name may be washed away to make peace, how much more would this apply to the honor of Rabbi Meir" (*Leviticus Rabbah* 10:9).

The urgent pursuit of peace is not necessarily equivalent to a position of pacifism. Jewish law distinguishes between different kinds of war which may merit different responses. It requires a person to support a war of self-defense which it terms a *milchemet mitzvah*, an "obligatory war." The rationale for a war of self-defense derives from the ethic of self-fulfillment. That ethical principle affirms the right of a person to protect his own well-being so long as he does not deny an equivalent right to other people. The right of a person to preserve his own life supersedes the claim of any other person to take that life. Every individual deserves the freedom to live in peace, as does every community. On that premise, Jewish law justifies a war of self-defense.

The teachers of Judaism also recognized, however, the possibility of a *milchemet r'shut*, an "optional war." Such combat was clearly a voluntary enterprise "to extend the borders of Israel and to enhance its greatness and prestige." It could be waged only with the explicit approval of the Great Sanhedrin of seventy-one sages; since that body has ceased to exist, the morality of a milchemet r'shut becomes wholly academic.

The problem of supporting a milchemet mitzvah is the resulting dilemma when both sides to a conflict claim that the cause of each is a matter of self-defense. An absolute pacifist would point out that neither side is entirely guilty or innocent, and that violence is therefore a repulsive alternative in any situation. The dominant thrust of rabbinic tradition, however, would sanction recourse to armed force in cases where an intended victim of aggession is bereft of any other option to defend himself or protect his interests.

Although pacifism is not a majority stance in Judaism, a significant strand of Jewish literature extols the virtue of nonviolence in any circumstance. It rests on the premise that all warfare is mass murder especially in this world that hovers on the brink of nuclear annihilation and that any discussion of humane rules of war is a contradiction in terms. A major source for this view is the teaching of the Mishnah that:

> Only one single person was created in the world to teach that, if any person has caused a single soul to perish, Scripture imputes it to him as if he had caused an entire world to perish; and if any person saves alive a single soul, Scripture imputes it to him as if he had saved a whole world. [*Sanhedrin* 4:5]

Other passages in the Talmud reinforce this reverence for nonviolence. Some urge you to help an enemy, because it will both control your own aggressive impulse and possibly touch your enemy's heart. Elsewhere we are told that the "hero of heroes" is the individual who turns an enemy into a friend. That feat far surpasses any military exploits. Still further, the Midrash emphasizes that when Jacob finally confronted the superior force of Esau on the eve of their reconciliation, Scripture records that Jacob simply sat down, posing no threat to Esau, and convinced his adversary that recourse to arms was unnecessary.

These teachings are clearly a minor theme on the subject of peace in Judaism, but they demonstrate decisively that pacifism was not a foreign notion to spiritual idealism in early Jewish tradition. Indeed in this age of potential nuclear catastrophe, it may become a dominant motif.

THE SABBATH

Not all mitzvot are manifestly ethical. Indeed, the vast majority belong to a second category which may be termed ritual or ceremonial mitzvot. In traditional Judaism, all mitzvot are equally binding, although they are not all of equal significance. Theoretically, the two categories are inseparable; but if in fact one is ever forced to choose, ethical injunctions transcend all others.

Nonetheless, ritual and ceremonial practice is usually a more helpful distinction between observant and nonobservant Jews. Religious and nonreligious Jews alike will subscribe to the moral requirements of Torah; only religious Jews will add the requirements of ritual and ceremony to their agenda. That is why an appreciation for the teachings of Torah necessarily includes an understanding of the ritual mitzvot. This category begins with an explanation of the holy day and festival cycle in Judaism.

The most important of all Jewish holy days is *Shabbat*, that is, the Sabbath. The Sabbath is perhaps the most eloquent illustration of the Jewish view of God and man. As we have already observed, Judaism teaches a belief in God that encourages people to achieve their greatest capacities as human beings. God does not contend against man, but pleads with him to utilize one day to activate the godliness that resides in him. Mankind is not distinguished by its labor; the simplest of animals works as diligently and sometimes more effectively than man. Man is not distinguished by his sensory equipment. Every living creature can see, hear, touch, taste, and smell almost as well as and sometimes more efficiently than human beings.

Judaism teaches and the Sabbath echoes the conviction that only man is distinguished by a soul, by a capacity to understand right and wrong, to seek truth, to perceive love and beauty, and to comprehend part of the ultimate mystery of creation. These comprise man's special claim to eminence, and these should be his concerns on the day of his rest. To deny or ignore the Sabbath is to deny the very purpose for which man was created.

The Sabbath makes every human being equal, regardless of his social, economic, or political status. Master and slave, rich and poor, scholar, and illiterate are all blessed with Sabbath peace, not as a concession from any human authority, but as a God-given right. Our tradition reminds us that it is man's inalienable right to be free. The Sabbath ideal of human equality resounds in the Talmud when it tells us:

> The rabbis of Yavneh used to say, "I am a human being, and so is my neighbor. My work is in the city, and his work is in the field. I rise early to do my work and he rises early to do his. Shall I say that I advance the cause of learning more than he does? We are taught that it matters not whether one offers much or little, so long as one's heart is directed toward heaven." [*Berachot* 17a]

The Sabbath is the only holiday in Judaism that is prescribed by the Ten Commandments. It is a weekly period of recreation and restoration. Part of its purpose is religious commitment, but part is also social responsibility. The rabbinic commentators explain the distinction in terms of the two different versions of the Decalogue (the Ten Commandments) in the Torah. In the earlier form in Exodus, the Sabbath is a continual reenactment of divine creation. On the Sabbath every person should strive to emulate divine attributes. That is the implication of the summons to "'remember the Sabbath day, to keep it holy . . . for in six days the Lord made heaven and earth [and] sea . . . and rested on the seventh day . . . and hallowed it'" (Exod. 20:8–11). Therefore, every person may sanctify the seventh day by resting on it and acting as God did. Most especially, the Exodus narrative focuses on God as the source of all blessing and good fortune in Whom the very mystery of life begins and ends.

In the account of Deuteronomy, however, the observance of the Sabbath is a reminder of the Exodus from Egypt. It is a reenactment of emancipation and a celebration of freedom. Creation is not enough to endow life with meaning and significance. Freedom is an indispensable component. Social justice and social conscience in Judaism are inseparable from their spiritual roots. All people deserve the rest and tranquility of the Sabbath, because they are all created in the same image of God. Belief in God requires social responsibility, and social responsibility stems from religious conviction. The Sabbath teaches that faith and action are indivisible.

The gift of the Sabbath is the unique contribution of Judaism to mankind. The entire body of social legislation in the Western world is based on it. For the Jewish people the Sabbath is the supreme symbol of the Covenant between God and themselves.

The Sabbath was not a day of gloom or depression; on the contrary, the Sabbath was a time for joy and delight. In describing the nature of all festivals, the Talmud stipulated: "Half is for God, half is for you" (*Betza* 15b). That formula meant that certain activities and categories of work were forbidden, and that service to God was paramount. It also meant, however, that food, drink, song, and pleasant recreation were all part of the Sabbath observance. Young men and women often anticipated their leisurely, private moments together on this day, and lovemaking in marriage was explicitly encouraged on the Sabbath.

The Sabbath, as well as all Jewish holidays, begins and ends at sundown. The rabbis noted that in the account of creation the text states, "There was evening and there was morning, the first day" (Gen. 1:5), which teaches that every twenty-four hour period begins with darkness and eventually yields to light. A more practical consideration might be the recognition that in an agrarian society, the day ends as night descends. Farmers would be more inclined to think and plan for the next day when they began their rest the previous night. Shabbat thus begins on Friday evening and continues to sundown on Saturday evening.

Shabbat arrives with a special mood on Friday evening at home. The house is neater, the children are cleaner, the pace is slower than on other evenings. The family is together. The dinner table is set in a more festive manner. The setting, of course, includes the major components of Sabbath observance—the candles, the wine, and the two loaves of *challah* (a twisted, braided bread loaf). A special blessing is recited or chanted over each of these symbols. The candles are a reminder of light which evokes allusions to truth, knowledge, goodness, justice, and peace. Proper observance includes at least two or more Sabbath candles, one for the ordinary light of every day, and additional light for the brightness of the Sabbath.

Wine in Judaism is always a symbol of joy. As the Psalmist declared, God made plants for man to grow for food and for "wine to gladden the heart of man" (Ps. 104:15). Since the Sabbath is an occasion of supreme joy, wine is a fitting choice for its celebration.

The same rationale explains the use of wine on numerous other occasions, including festivals, *b'rit milah* (circumcision), *bar* and *bat mitzvah*, and weddings.

The blessing over bread is a regular feature that precedes every meal, but on the Sabbath this routine ritual is often enhanced with the addition of a guest or visitor for the festive dinner. The meal continues at a leisurely pace, interlaced with thoughtful conversation and zestful singing, and concludes with the usual custom of *birkat hamazon* ("grace after meals").

Although traditionally the time for Sabbath eve worship preceded the festive meal at sundown, in more liberal circles Sabbath eve worship is scheduled for the entire family after the dinner hour. This innovation was designed to accommodate those who were unable to participate at the earlier service on Friday evening or in the morning service on Saturday. Frequently the late Friday evening service is followed in the synagogue by an *Oneg Shabbat* (a social collation with food and discussion or song). In traditional Judaism, the major worship service on Shabbat remains on Saturday morning when the Torah is usually read and discussed.

The Sabbath day is devoted to worship, learning, reading, thoughtful reflection in the company of family and friends, and refreshing leisure that enhances the quality of ordinary living, such as a brisk walk on the beach, a stroll through the woods, or a hike in the mountains. It may be a time for visiting the sick, the lonely, the bereaved. It is even time for a quiet, restful nap, which the sages termed "a delight." As in Judaism generally, so on Shabbat specifically, earthly pleasures were never excluded from the realm of spirituality.

Just as the Sabbath began with a special ceremony of welcome at sunset on Friday, so the Sabbath ends with a special ceremony of farewell at sundown on Saturday. The ritual marking the division is called *havdalah*, which means "separation" and refers to the separation of the Sabbath day from all other days of the week. The wine cup is filled again as it was on Friday evening, and a braided candle is kindled. This time the candle's flame symbolizes the light of creation that appeared on the first day of the week, and the wine again is a reference to the joy of creation. The havdalah ceremony also includes a blessing over fragrant spices symbolizing the "aroma" of the Sabbath, which a Jew prays will remain and reinforce him for the week ahead.

The Jewish people measured all their time in terms of the Sabbath. Each day of the week was significant for its distance from the Sabbath. Each day was lived in anticipation of the Sabbath. The Sabbath was a weekly glimpse into the Messianic Age, a foretaste of the "world to come." A contemporary writer astutely observed, "More than Israel has kept the Sabbath, has the Sabbath kept Israel" (Ahad HaAm, *HaShiloah,* 1898, iii, 6).

THE HIGH HOLY DAYS

The beginning and end of the Jewish day is geared to the routines of ordinary farmers and workers. When their labor is done, their day is done. Evening then is the natural beginning for a new cycle of time.

The same pattern applies to the calendation for the entire year. For those who tend the soil, the year is over when the harvest is in. That is why the new year in the Hebrew calendar begins in the fall. This is a pattern that has remained unalterably fixed for centuries and remains one of the unique features of Judaism. All festivals and holy days retain their roots in an agricultural community, regardless of profound changes in time and place; and their observance is linked to living patterns in the land of Israel, even though the vast majority of Jews live elsewhere. Aside from any other significance, this is more than ample evidence for the centrality of the Land of Israel in the scale of Jewish values.

The first ten days of the Hebrew calendar are known collectively as the Ten Days of Repentance. It is a very solemn period, a time for serious reflection and self-assessment. These days begin on the first day of the month of Tishri which is *Rosh Hashanah,* the "New Year," and culminate on the tenth day, *Yom Kippur,* or the "Day of Atonement." These are such eminently sacred occasions that Jews address them as the High Holy Days.

An extraordinary feature of the Jewish New Year is its computation of time based not on any significant event in the history of the

Jewish people, but on the act of creation according to biblical calculation, an event significant to all mankind. The Hebrew calendar is the reflection of a universal message for all peoples, not just Jews.

Judaism teaches that everything a person does is recorded in a book of life for good or for evil. Tradition stipulates that the accounting procedure is supervised directly by God, or, according to some sources, by Elijah the prophet, who acts on God's behalf. At the beginning of the New Year, the book is opened for the examination of every individual record. Every person's deeds are judged and weighed. A verdict is reached and inscribed. The judgment, however, is not permanently sealed until Yom Kippur. The final decision may be tempered with mercy for those who truly correct their ways and resolve to improve their conduct in the coming year. This sacred season is not simply a time for resignation to an arbitrary, divine decree. It is a resounding reassurance that God will forgive any wrongdoing if a person is serious about changing. Even though every individual is conditioned by his own peculiar circumstances, Jewish faith is predicated on the conviction that prayer, repentance, and good deeds can alter the verdict of Rosh Hashanah.

The most instructive symbol of Rosh Hashanah is the sounding of the *shofar*, a ram's horn. The origins of the shofar ritual are steeped in layers of mysticism and homiletical interpretations that have accumulated over centuries. In more recent times, the sounding of the shofar is an invigorating reminder of the serious, personal assessment which the Days of Repentance demand of its adherents.

In the company of family and friends at home, the observance of Rosh Hashanah emphasizes the spirit of hope which the holy day symbolizes. In addition to the *kiddush*, the sanctification with wine, which is a symbol of joy for the New Year even as it is on the Sabbath, the standard Sabbath bread has been sweetened with a generous quantity of raisins. The head of the household also distributes to everyone assembled a piece of apple dipped in honey to reflect the wish that the coming year may be filled with sweetness and all good things.

In Orthodox communities, the afternoon of Rosh Hashanah includes a walk to a flowing body of water, such as a river or the seashore. There the participants sprinkle breadcrumbs over the water as a gesture of confidence that just as the tide or the current washes the breadcrumbs away, so will God wash away the sins of all those who sincerely repent. Since Orthodox and Conservative Jews observe Rosh Hashanah for two days, this ceremony occurs on the second day, if the first day falls on the Sabbath. Even the sounding of the shofar is not permitted on the Sabbath. Both activities are considered a form of work, which is forbidden on Shabbat.

No day of the year is as sacred or solemn in the Hebrew calendar as Yom Kippur, the Day of Atonement, and culmination of the Ten Days of Repentance. It is the only holy day which supersedes the Sabbath in importance, which is why it is frequently described as "the Sabbath of Sabbaths." The greeting of the High Holy Day season, *L'shanah tovah tikatevu*, "May you be inscribed for a good year," is especially meaningful at this hour.

On the eve of Yom Kippur Jews gather in their synagogues to begin an entire day of fasting and prayer. Explanations abound for the purpose of fasting; all of them are attempts to understand the meaning of the biblical injunction that on this day "you shall afflict yourselves . . ." (Lev. 16:29). One source explains that on Yom Kippur, every person should concentrate entirely on matters of the spirit to the exclusion of material needs. Moreover, this temporary self-deprivation which one inflicts upon one's self voluntarily improves one's sensitivity to the constant deprivation, hardship and abuse which many suffer at the hands of tyrants and political demagogues.

The interior of the synagogue is dominated by white as a symbol of purity. The Torah mantles, the pulpit robes, the lectern covers, and sometimes even the ark curtain are changed from their ordinary colors to white. The vision of purity and innocence stems from the scriptural assurance, "Though your sins are like scarlet, they shall be as white as snow. . . ." (Isa. 1:18).

The Yom Kippur eve service begins with a prayer called *Kol Nidre*. This exquisite spiritual statement is simply a declaration of dispensation from personal vows between man and God that were intended as special acts of piety and then broken. It does not invalidate any contractual pledges which one person seals with another. The haunting melody for this prayer, which became the musical theme for the evening service, conveys the longing of the human soul for its Creator, reflects on the sorrows and adversities of the year just ended, and in its closing passages ascends to majestic heights of courage and faith.

Throughout the day of Yom Kippur every individual recites his or her confessional personally before God and anticipates pardon directly from God. Every Jew is a priest of his or her own accord. Repentance and atonement require no intermediary in Judaism.

Nonetheless, the language of the prayer book stresses the plural far more than the singular pronoun. The petition almost always seeks forgiveness not for "me," but for "us," signifying that the destiny of every individual is inseparable from that of the entire congregation, or even of mankind as a whole. Jewish thought contends that even though every person is individually accountable, all people are mutually responsible.

The concluding service for Yom Kippur day is known as *N'ilah,* which means "closing" and referred originally to the closing of the Temple gates in Jerusalem at the end of the Day of Atonement. Gradually it evolved into a reference to the gates of heaven which were about to close; thus it symbolizes the last opportunity for a final appeal for mercy and forgiveness.

As the service ends, the shofar is sounded once again as the assurance of a new beginning of the spirit. The congregation responds with a chorus of hope that next year may find them all in Jerusalem. Yom Kippur is thus concluded.

THE MAJOR PILGRIM FESTIVALS

According to rabbinic literature, the preparations for the next festival of *Sukkoth* (the Feast of Tabernacles) begin with the close of Yom Kippur. The same evening, after the fast has been broken, the Jew is summoned to drive the first stakes into the ground for the building of the *sukkah,* the small, frail temporary hut that serves as the central symbol for this next major holiday.

The Hebrew calendar includes the celebration of three major festivals. Originally all were agricultural feast days marking the completion of a harvest period. They were also called pilgrim festivals, because they embraced the requirement of a pilgrimage to the Temple at Jerusalem as a display of thanksgiving for the bountiful blessings God has provided. In the course of time, each festival also developed a primary association with a climactic event in the history of the Jewish people. Thus, Sukkoth became synonymous with the event of the wandering through the wilderness, *Pesach* (Passover) with the emancipation from slavery in Egypt, and *Shavuoth* (Pentecost) with the theophany (revelation) at Sinai.

The Torah designated the first and last days of Sukkoth and Pesach (the first and last two days in Orthodox and Conservative Judaism) as "holy convocations" which preclude any ordinary labor but specify a particular liturgy for the festival. Among traditionally observant Jews, Shavuoth is celebrated for two days instead of one and is also a "holy convocation."

Sukkoth

The first of these festivals in the chronological order of the Hebrew calendar year is Sukkoth, which follows Yom Kippur by five days on the fifteenth day of Tishri. Every symbol and lesson of this holiday heightens the consciousness of every Jew to the marvels of nature and the world he or she lives in. In the modern idiom, Sukkoth is a superb holiday of homage to the principles of ecology.

Sukkoth represented the ingathering of the fall harvest in biblical times. As the Jewish people evolved through history from a community of farmers to a community of scholars and city-dwellers, their festivals reminded them continuously of their humble origins in the world of nature from which they were drifting considerably with the passage of time. Sukkoth therefore is truly a holiday for modern man, because it is a glorification of earlier, simpler times in sharp contrast to the present world of advancing technology in which ever-increasing walls threaten to shut out all mankind from any contact with nature itself.

The Covenant designates Sukkoth as *Hechag*—"The Festival." Speculation abounds that the sages assigned this name to the holiday, because it embodies the essential values of Jewish living. Two important symbols dominate Sukkoth. The first is the frail, temporary hut in which the celebrants dine for the duration of the holiday. It is erected in remembrance of the rapidly built and collapsible shelters required in the desert wanderings. Two of the foremost philosophers, Philo and Maimonides, challenged this explanation however. They taught that the small, unstable structure helped to accentuate for the comfortable, prosperous Jew the misfortunes of those in poverty and despair. The tenuous quality of the sukkah was a visual statement that the security of physical possessions is totally unreliable. The only permanent security is the imperishable bonds a person builds with other people and with the elements of the natural world. This penetrating message of Sukkoth has inspired increasing numbers of Jews in recent years to build their own sukkahs outside their homes and apartments. The effort enables them to appreciate constantly throughout the entire eight-day period of the festival the delights of outdoor living from which they have become so sadly estranged and insulated by growing urbanization and the mechanization of a technological civilization.

The second major symbol of Sukkoth is a set of four objects from nature. First is the *ethrog* (''citron''). The Midrash suggests that the ethrog, since it has both taste and aroma, represents those Jews who have both knowledge of Torah and perform good deeds. The other three items are bound together and known by the name of the largest item, the *lulav* (''palm branch''). The palm branch, which has taste but no aroma, represents those Jews who know Torah but do not perform good deeds. The *hadassah,* a branch of myrtle leaves attached to the lulav, has aroma but not taste and therefore represents Jews who perform good deeds but understand nothing of Torah. Finally, the *aravah,* a branch of willow leaves attached to the lulav, possesses neither taste nor aroma and thus symbolizes Jews without Torah or good deeds. The lulav and ethrog are held and carried together at home and in the synagogue with the recitation of appropriate blessings for each.

Following the last day of Sukkoth is the holiday of *Shemini Atzeret,* the eighth day of assembly, which returns the focus of the festival from the home to the synagogue.

Simchat Torah

Reform Jewish congregations usually combine the last day of Sukkoth with the observance of *Shemini Atzeret* and *Simchat Torah,* an occasion for rejoicing over the Covenant's heritage. This is the time the annual cycle of the reading of the Torah scroll is completed. The prevailing custom consists of a reading from the final verses of Deuteronomy followed immediately by a reading from the opening lines of the Book of Genesis. This ceremony stresses the unbroken chain of tradition as well as the precept that the learning process never ends but continues for a lifetime.

Simchat Torah is a celebration of abounding energy, joy, and enthusiasm that is designed for the entire family. The leaders of the service customarily distribute flags to the children and invite the whole congregation to march in festive procession with the Torah scrolls around the entire sanctuary. Everyone participates in singing and sometimes even dancing, and several people are honored by being called to the pulpit to recite the appropriate blessings over the Torah.

Through its ceremonies and observances, Sukkoth thus incorporates an abundance of basic Jewish ideals, including love of learning, the return to nature, and sensitivity to the needs of all living things. In this context it is not difficult to appreciate why the rabbis equate Sukkoth with Hechag—The Festival.

Pesach (Passover)

The second major festival in the Hebrew calendar is *Pesach,* or Passover. Like the other two pilgrim festivals, Pesach was originally an agricultural feast day which initiated the early harvest period in Palestine. The first ripened barley grains were cut on Passover and offered in thanksgiving at the Temple in Jerusalem.

Passover, however, is also the supreme festival of freedom. It is the Emancipation Proclamation for the Jewish people, the Independence Day of Jewish history. It is similar to other freedom celebrations and yet distinctively different, because it attributed the gift of freedom not to any human agency but to God alone. Only God could endow mankind with "inalienable rights" to life, liberty, and the pursuit of duty as well as happiness. No human authority could ever confer these rights or revoke them. They belonged to all people by virtue of their divine endowment.

The central message of Passover is the proposition that the Jews were redeemed from slavery in Egypt not just for the sake of their own independence, but for the sake of promoting the cause of freedom for all peoples. That is why the freedom of Passover is incomplete until the Messianic Age and the future redemption of all people who still suffer from oppression and tyranny.

The story of Pesach clearly implies that the Jewish people could not have appreciated freedom unless they had first endured the bitterness of slavery. The Covenant is rooted in these painful, humble beginnings. In Judaism, it is no disgrace to be a slave; it is only a disgrace to enslave others.

Passover is the most colorful and captivating of all Jewish holidays. It celebrates not only the supreme significance of human freedom, but also the rebirth of nature, compassion for the disadvantaged, and hope for a radiant future.

The most visible symbol of Pesach is the *matzah*—unleavened bread. During their enslavement in Egypt, the Jews seldom had sufficient time to complete the bread-baking process. They were forced to flee in haste and to depart with unleavened bread, which was thus termed "the bread of affliction." Because of its association with the flight from Egypt, matzah became the Jews' symbolic food of freedom.

Only matzah and other unleavened products may be consumed for the duration of Passover. All leavened foods are strictly forbidden for the period of seven days it took the Israelites to cross the Red Sea and finally escape from their Egyptian enemies. The Torah stipulates that the holiday shall be observed for seven days, although in traditional Jewish circles it continues for eight days because of early difficulties in determining the accuracy of the calendar. The first days, which recount the actual departure, and the last days, which mark the assurance of freedom from slavery, are major observances which include abstention from work and worship services in the synagogue. The intervening days, which correspond to the period of traveling, are minor festive occasions.

Because all leavened foods are strictly forbidden on Passover, many observant Jews will conduct a symbolic search of their homes to ensure that no trace of *chametz* ("leaven") remains anywhere on the premises. In addition, they will replace all their dishes and cooking utensils for the duration of the holiday to avoid any possible contamination of Passover foods with ordinary kitchenware.

The major celebration in the observance of Passover is the *seder,* the ritual meal and service on the first and second evenings of Pesach. *Seder* means "order" and refers to the order of service the participants follow in observing the festive meal. The procedure for conducting the seder is fully detailed in a guide for this purpose called the Haggadah ("the Story"). The story of Passover in the Haggadah begins with a review of the earliest events in Jewish history and culminates in a projection of the future Messianic Age when the liberation of all oppressed peoples will complete the emancipation of Israel in its Exodus from Egypt.

The seder meal and service include the consumption of four glasses of wine, each corresponding to a different expression of redemption in the biblical account of the event. In the center of the table is placed a separate additional cup to symbolize a fifth promise of redemption, which alludes to the ultimate liberation of all mankind from all forms of tyranny. Because the messenger entrusted with the mission of proclaiming the coming of the messianic world on God's behalf is Elijah the prophet, this separate goblet is called the Cup of Elijah. It is not consumed by anyone, but emphasizes the truth that with sufficient effort and determination, the redemption of the future can become as much a reality as that of the past.

At the very beginning of the seder service, every participant dips a sprig of parsley into salt water as a joyful symbol of springtime, but also as a reminder of the tears our ancestors shed in their painful plight. This blend of joy and sadness is a major component of every significant Jewish observance and underscores the precept that life is always a bittersweet fusion of both victories and defeats, of hope as well as despair.

The central element in the observance of the seder is family participation. Even in homes which minimize the use of the Haggadah, Pesach is still the occasion for a family gathering. The Haggadah itself is designed deliberately to evoke and maintain the interest of children. The Mishnah advises the leader of the service to proceed quickly with the narrative, especially on the first night, to keep the level of interest high among the youngsters. At the heart of the service are the four questions relating to the unique features of the seder which the youngest child is instructed to ask. Jewish law stipulates that the seder must conclude with the eating of a portion of matzah called the *afikomen* ("dessert"). No food may be consumed after this course. In addition it is customary, though not mandatory, to hide a portion of afikomen matzah which the children are sent to find and redeem for a prize before the seder officially concludes.

Passover proclaims a timeless message at every level of Jewish observance, including its synagogue ritual, its home ceremonies, and personal practice. It is essentially a celebration of springtime, a season of rebirth and renewal, a time for rededication to the sublime meaning of freedom and emancipation from every vestige of human tyranny. Pesach is an eternal lesson about the supreme priority of life, hope, and redemption for all mankind.

Shavuoth (Pentecost)

The last of the three major festivals in Judaism also originated as a celebration of an abundant harvest and then evolved into a holiday of historical dimension. The feast of Shavuoth occurs in late spring and also ranks as a pilgrim festival, deserving of a visit to the Temple in Jerusalem. The name of the holiday is the Hebrew term for "weeks," which is a fitting designation, because it follows seven weeks after Pesach. It is again a reminder of the attachment of our people to the land of their origins and their total dependence on the soil for their well-being.

Shavuoth conveys a message not only about nature but also about the world of spiritual reality. It is especially significant with reference to the Covenant, because it commemorates the revelation of Torah at Mt. Sinai. This association explains the particular significance of its observance in modern times.

Many synagogues schedule their confirmation ceremonies on or close to Shavuoth. The ritual is often incorporated into the standard festival worship service, which is developed and led by young people who have completed their formal religious education through the junior high level or beyond and who publicly declare their attachments to Judaism and the Jewish people. Despite the wide diversity of confirmation ceremonies from one synagogue to another, all offer a resounding reaffirmation of the Torah by both parents and children which embodies the essence of Jewish faith and loyalty. Just as Moses received the Torah at Sinai, according to tradition, so every generation of young people reenacts that historic moment by receiving and accepting the Torah on Shavuoth.

Confirmation originated as an innovation of Reform Judaism in the early nineteenth century, and was based on the principle of equal status and equal rights for men and women. It began in many Reform congregations as a replacement for bar and bat mitzvah observance, but gradually became an additional ceremony at the high school level, equivalent to a graduation from religious school. In more recent times, confirmation has become not so much a statement of obedience to Judaism as a statement of a continuing search for fulfillment in Judaism. The ceremony is no longer limited to Reform congregations, but has been adopted by most Conservative synagogues and by some Orthodox synagogues as well.

Shavuoth remains a festival of reconsecration to the timeless teachings of Torah and to the endless quest for new insight into its larger meaning. To that extent it is a constant reminder of the significance of the Covenant.

THE MINOR FESTIVALS

The calendar cycle of holidays in Judaism also includes a series of minor festivals. They are considered minor not because they are necessarily less meaningful than other holidays, but primarily because they do not include any special liturgies or the major categories of prohibited activities associated with other festivals.

Hanukkah

Probably the most popular of all these minor holidays is *Hanukkah*. Hanukkah is *not* the "Jewish Christmas." Actually, Christmas is the "Christian Hanukkah." Hanukkah has become increasingly significant in recent times, not simply because of its proximity to the Christian holiday of Christmas, but because of the message it proclaims in support of religious freedom and in opposition to the temptations of assimilation.

Hanukkah is a celebration of the first recorded battle in the history of mankind for freedom of conscience. The name of the festival means "dedication." It refers not so much to the military victory of the Maccabees over the Greek-Syrian tyranny, but to the rededication of the Temple which had been defiled by the enemy as a pagan shrine. Hanukkah is not a victory celebration in the usual sense. It focuses far more upon the triumph of righteousness than of armed might. The most fitting summation of its message is the statement from the *haftarah* (prophetic portion) assigned for the Sabbath during the holiday which proclaims: "Not by might, nor by power, but by My spirit, says the Lord of hosts." (Zech. 4:6).

The historical account of the events which culminated in this observance began approximately in 165 B.C.E. when King Antiochus Epiphanes IV ordered that a pagan altar be erected at the Temple in Jerusalem and that sacrifices be prepared in homage to Zeus. Most Jews capitulated to the royal injunction; but a small band of determined dissenters, led by the Maccabee family, retreated to the countryside and began a continuing campaign of sporadic assaults and skirmishes. They battled not only the external enemy, but even the sizable portion of their own Jewish community which found the appeal of Greek culture irresistible. Eventually, their tactics and persistence totally frustrated and exhausted their most powerful opposition, so that they were able to recapture Jerusalem and repossess their sacred Temple site.

They proceeded to purify the Temple from its pagan ritual beginning on the twenty-fifth day of the Hebrew month of Kislev. The Talmud reports that at that time the Maccabees, who later became the founders of the Hasmonean royal dynasty, thoroughly searched the sanctuary and finally found one small cruse of oil still bearing the seal of the high priest. There was just enough oil to last for one day in the holy candelabrum of the Temple. But, we are told, a miracle happened, and it burned for eight days until new, properly prepared oil could be produced. The following year it was ordained that "these days should be observed with songs of praise and thanksgiving" (*Shabbat* 21b).

It is also possible, if not likely, that Hanukkah evolved into an observance of eight days in tribute to the festival of Sukkoth which was the holiday closest in proximity to the recapture of Jerusalem. Since Sukkoth was designed precisely as a holiday of thanksgiving, a better model could not possibly be found for this most recent occasion of rejoicing.

The candles which are lit on each successive night of Hanukkah were originally placed outdoors as a symbol of the victory of light over darkness. Because of relentless persecutions and pogroms, however, Jews were compelled to restrict the lighting of candles to the privacy of their own homes. The special candelabrum for the holiday is called a *hanukiyah;* it consists of eight branches, one for each succeeding night, and a ninth branch, higher than the rest, which functions as the *shamash* (servant) candle with which the others are kindled.

A debate in the Talmud between two great sages, Hillel and Shammai, revolved about the question of whether the hanukiyah should begin with eight brightly burning candles on the first night and gradually decrease to a single flickering flame, as Shammai taught, or whether it should begin with one candle and eventually finish with eight, as Hillel taught, based on the premise that one should always increase and magnify the observance of a mitzvah and never decrease it. Hillel's view prevailed, and has been the practice in all Jewish communities to the present day.

Hanukkah is a time of joy and excitement, particularly for children. Games, plays, and special foods, especially *latkes* ("potato pancakes"), all contribute to an unusually festive mood. In recent years, the practice of exchanging gifts has grown rapidly, both from the Jewish custom of receiving *Hanukkah gelt* ("holiday coins") and also as a result of the commercialization of Christmas.

For the modern Jew, however, Hanukkah's significance far surpasses candle lighting, gifts for children, or latkes. The primary principle is the sanctity of individual conscience, and the right of every person to choose his or her own faith without interference from any political authority. Faith must be founded in the freedom to worship in whatever style best suits the needs and longings of every human soul. Although it technically is relegated to the status of a minor holiday, Hanukkah still addresses a major theme of the civilized world for Jews and non-Jews alike.

Purim

Just as Hanukkah commemorates the first successful struggle for the survival of Judaism, the festival of *Purim* represents the first successful struggle for the survival of the Jewish people. *Purim* is the Hebrew term for "lots," and refers to the method by which the date was chosen to destroy the Jews of ancient Persia.

The story of Purim is based on the biblical narrative in the Book of Esther. It is a remarkable legend with an abundance of heroes and villains who evoke associations with a host of unforgettable personalities in ordinary experience. Mordecai is the grandest hero of all, risking his life to thwart those determined to eliminate his people. Esther, his grandniece, is also a paragon of courage who eventually intercedes with the king on her people's behalf. Haman is the personification of evil as the pernicious, diabolical prime minister who masterminds the extermination of the Jews without divulging his conspiracy to King Ahasuerus or the rejected Queen Vashti.

Even though the tale is more fiction than fact, subsequent historical events certainly substantiated the belief that the Purim episode is a paradigm of the threats and mortal dangers which repeatedly assailed the Jewish people in every generation. The story of oppression and persecution in Jewish experience is too familiar to be a myth. The joyous conclusion in the Book of Esther was a constant beacon of hope and encouragement in the darkest and most dismal of times.

Because of its actual historical associations, Purim is one of the most popular of all Jewish holidays. The ritual observance of this minor festival is exceedingly modest. There is no home observance, and the synagogue celebration is limited to the chanting or recitation of the *Megillah* (the Book of Esther in the form of a "scroll"). The accompanying mood almost approaches a carnival atmosphere. It is customary to drown out the name of Haman, the villain, each time his name is mentioned by ringing noisemakers, greggers, pots, pans, and by foot stomping. In the same way, the people respond with applause and cheering every time the name Mordecai or Esther is read.

In addition to the Megillah reading, Purim is also a time for dramatic parodies, masquerades, and games of chance. Children frequently dress up in costume and reenact the events in the Book of Esther. Among adults, Purim is the only occasion when drinking is permissible; it continues until one cannot distinguish between the goodness of Mordecai and the wickedness of Haman.

One of the most familiar symbols of Purim is its special three-cornered pastry, called *hamantaschen*, which in Yiddish means "pockets of poppy seeds." The name probably refers also to the villain in the Purim story, because the Hebrew name for the pastry, *oznat haman*, means "the ears of Haman."

Finally, Purim is also a time for tzedakah, acts of righteousness. In the context of this holiday, the responsibility entails the practice of *shalach manot*, sending gifts of food to friends and to people in need. Indeed, the donor never embarrasses a recipient by designating his gift for the poor. One is expected to give because the beneficiary is a friend, not an economic burden.

T'u B'Shevat

The remaining observances of ritual mitzvoth in terms of the holiday cycle are relatively modest but nonetheless significant for the Jewish ideals they reflect.

T'u B'Shevat, which refers to the Hebrew calendar date of *Chamisha Assar B'Shevat* (''the fifteenth day of Shevat''), is so designated because the Hebrew letters *tet* and *vov,* T and U, add up to a total of fifteen. The festival is essentially the New Year of Trees, a source perhaps of the later Arbor Day, and more currently an ecology observance. Especially in Israel, but everywhere else in the Jewish world as well, it is an occasion for planting trees and emphasizing human responsibility for preserving the natural environment. It is customary also to eat fruits imported from Israel or those varieties grown in Israel, such as figs, dates, pomegranates, and especially, the carob bean, known in English as ''Saint John's Bread'' and in Yiddish as *bokser.*

Lag B'Omer

Lag B'Omer means literally ''thirty-three in the measure.'' In their early agrarian development, Jews celebrated the harvest of the very first sheaf of barley by bringing this *omer,* the first ''measure,'' as an offering of thanks on the second day of Passover. They then counted forty-nine days, seven full weeks, and on the fiftieth day they observed Shavuoth, the Feast of Weeks. Lag B'Omer is an observance that occurs on the thirty-third day in this seven-week cycle.

The Bible does not mention this holiday at all. One legend explains its observance as the one day of relief during a most tragic period of seven weeks. A terrible epidemic is reported to have claimed the lives of many students of Rabbi Akiba in the second century. The epidemic stopped suddenly on Lag B'Omer, and Rabbi Akiba survived with all his remaining students.

Another legend attributes its origins to the miraculous survival of Judaism during a severe persecution in the time of Akiba. After the Romans destroyed Jerusalem and the Temple in the year 70, they banned the study or teaching of Judaism on penalty of death. One of the scholars who defied the Roman order was Rabbi Simeon ben Yohai. He and his son hid themselves in a cave and studied there in secret for thirteen years. Several of their students often visited and studied with them. Simeon ben Yohai urged his disciples not to mourn on the day of his death, but to celebrate it in remembrance of his life. That day occurred on Lag B'Omer, and in Israel Jews still observe this festival with a visit to the place where he presumably is buried.

Lag B'Omer is primarily a children's holiday. Hebrew school students enjoy a holiday from classes and often go on picnics and hikes. Some even carry bows and arrows in emulation of Simeon's disciples.

In a few places the occasion is also the observance of Jewish Book Day in tribute to the reverence for learning of all Rabbi Simeon's disciples.

Since the period of seven weeks between Passover and Shavuoth was filled with adversity and hardship, the scheduling of weddings is strictly forbidden among Conservative and Orthodox Jews. The only exception during this lengthy time is Lag B'Omer, which accounts for the abundance of marriage ceremonies scheduled for this day.

Tisha B'Ab

The ninth day of the month of Ab is observed as a major fast from sundown to sundown. On that day, known as *Tisha B'Ab* ("ninth of Ab"), the first Temple was destroyed by the Babylonians in 586 B.C.E. and then later by the Romans in 70 C.E. According to an ancient tradition, the ninth of Ab was also the day on which Moses descended from Mt. Sinai to witness his people worshipping the golden calf, whereupon he smashed the tablets of the Decalogue which God had given him.

Many other tragedies and disasters in Jewish history reportedly occurred on this date. They include the expulsion from Spain in 1492, pogroms in Russia, and the most terrifying mass murders and calamities in Nazi Germany. For example, *Kristalnacht*, "The Night of Broken Glass," occurred on November 9, 1938. Thus this particular day is reserved for grief and mourning.

In the synagogue, the most observant Jews worship while sitting on the floor. The decorative curtain is removed from the ark; the service includes a special Torah portion (Deuteronomy 4:25–50), a selection from the prophet Jeremiah (8:13–9:23), and the entire Book of Lamentations. The liturgy also contains references to the medieval massacres of Jewish communities.

In addition to the observance of ritual mitzvoth for the holidays already discussed, recent events in world history have stimulated the development of new observances in the festival and holiday cycle. This is not surprising in terms of honoring the Covenant as a living document.

In the first place, the religious significance of all Jewish festivals is rooted in a collective experience of the past. The association of the Exodus with Passover, of the wilderness wandering with Sukkoth, of the revelation at Sinai with Shavuoth, even of the Hasmonean Revolt with Hanukkah, is more than ample evidence that Jewish holidays evolve out of climactic, historical events.

Secondly, we have already emphasized the fundamental precept in Judaism that every person is a partner with God in renewing continuously the process of Creation. The expansion of the festival calendar is therefore a reflection of that confidence in the energy and vitality of an ancient Covenant in a modern world.

Yom Hashoah

A new holiday in this category is *Yom Hashoah* ("Holocaust Memorial Day"). Yom Hashoah is observed in Israel on the twenty-seventh of the Hebrew month of *Nisan,* which falls usually in April between the beginning of the Warsaw ghetto uprising on the first day of Passover in 1942 and the outbreak of Israel's War for Independence on the third of *Iyar* in 1948. The date is also significant because it occurs during the traditional period of mourning in the *Sefirah* ("Counting of the Omer"), the period between Passover and Shavuoth which refers especially to the commandments of offering the *omer* ("the sheaf of the first fruits") in the ancient Temple sanctuary on the second day of Passover.

In Israel places of entertainment are closed on Yom Hashoah, and sirens are sounded in memory of the six million martyrs of the Nazi era, 1933–1945. Outside Israel, the observance in worship and memorial tributes is usually reserved for April 19, which was the date in the civil calendar on which the Warsaw ghetto uprising broke out.

Yom Ha-atzmauth

Another new holiday is *Yom Ha-atzmauth* (Israel Independence Day). Yom Ha-atzmauth is celebrated in Israel on the fifth of Iyar, which is the anniversary of the day on May 14, 1948, when the Jewish settlement in Palestine proclaimed its Declaration of Independence and reestablished the State of Israel after 1,878 years of statelessness. The day is observed in Israel with dancing in the streets, fireworks displays, and picnic trips to the countryside, as well as official ceremonies and open-air entertainments. The day is also recognized in religious circles as a Jewish festival. Festive worship services are held in synagogues throughout the country and are highlighted by visits from cabinet ministers and other government leaders.

In Jewish communities throughout the world, Yom Ha-atzmauth is an occasion for demonstrating support for and solidarity with Israel as a central element of Jewish existence. The celebration in the Diaspora is also a time for rejoicing in the progress and achievements of the young state in its brief history.

WORSHIP

The performance of ritual mitzvoth in fulfillment of the Covenant is not limited to the celebration of holy days and festivals. It includes a wide range of ceremonial observance, much of which involves the duty of worship.

Communal prayer, or worship, in Judaism is as old as the Covenant itself. It began with reports of biblical episodes such as that of Abraham's petition to God on behalf of Sodom and Gomorrah (Gen. 18:22–33) or the appeal of Moses on behalf of all the people of Israel (Exodus 33—34).

Although Jewish prayer may be spontaneous, prompted entirely by the longings of the heart, as was the prayer of Hannah for the child she hoped to conceive (I Sam. 1:1–13), the rabbinic sages specified prescribed periods during the day for worship. They based such a directive on a family analogy in which a person may easily forget a parent who is not always visible without an opportunity for regular reminders. A person may also forget the most essential ideals that inspire his or her life without a periodic review of their meaning and purpose. Prayer that is left to a moment of sudden whim or impulse may never occur at all. In the same way excessive worship often leads to triviality and triteness.

The architects of Jewish worship always emphasized the difference between a warm intimacy with God and irreverent familiarity. The Talmud warned, "When you pray, always remember before Whom you stand" (*Berachot* 28b). In scolding those who make their worship a perfunctory exercise, it further added, "A person who regards praying simply as a duty to be performed, his prayer ceases to be supplication" (*Berachot* 4:4). Worship requires the concentration of the entire person without the interruption of any external distraction. The rabbis taught: "Even if the king should greet him, the worshipper may not interrupt his prayer to return the greeting" (*Berachot* 5:1). The character of Jewish worship is a blend of this formal rubric of fixed liturgy, continually renewed with original and spontaneous impulses of the heart.

The Jewish prayer book is the most informative one-volume history of Judaism available. It is a veritable composite of Jewish experience from its biblical roots to contemporary sources. It reflects every period of Jewish existence and the response of the people to those periods. In times of great hope and promise, the prayer book overflowed with songs of praise and thanksgiving. In times of adversity and oppression, it echoed the heartache and agony of a people who refused to despair. The worshipper can find in its pages evidence of every significant episode in the Jewish march through history.

The prayer book is also the daily guide for every ordinary Jew. The Talmud is the domain of scholars, an entire library of learning difficult to explore without intensive training. The prayer book, however, is the general property of every worshipper, however well or poorly educated.

It specifies the exact times for prayer and what prayers to recite on every important occasion. The Mishnah stipulates the recitation of the Shema, the affirmation of God's unity containing introductory and succeeding blessings, every morning and every evening. The Talmud further provides for a collection of eighteen benedictions, known as the *T'filah* ("the Prayer") or the *Sh'monah Esreh* (''the Eighteen''), to be recited morning, afternoon, and evening; these are slightly modified to accommodate the worship theme of the Sabbath or any of the other holidays.

The pattern of Jewish worship was already firmly established by the time of earliest Christianity. The Gregorian chants of the Roman Catholic and Eastern Orthodox churches are vestiges of early synagogue cantillations. Certain segments of the Mass embody the earliest components of Jewish liturgy.

The continuity of the prayer book, in the face of enormous political and social upheaval, is itself an astounding phenomenon. Jewish communities usually maintained sufficient contact despite the most severe stresses and strains to ensure a basic similarity in their respective liturgies. Jews of Spain and Portugal added their own poetic selections to their holiday services; the Jews of France and Germany added their variations, as did their peers in Poland and Russia.

In more recent times, prayer books have been published with translations and commentaries in the native language of each country. Even without a prayer book, the observant Jew who enters a synagogue anywhere in the world may quickly detect a familiarity with both the prayers and the mood of the service he attends.

The most noticeable changes in worship have been made by the Reform or ''liberal'' movement. Since the early nineteenth century, Reform prayer books have been published in German, French, and English, as well as in Hebrew. Most of these volumes eliminate repetitions of the Orthodox service and delete references to the restoration of the sacrificial cult in Jerusalem, the bodily resurrection of the dead, and the advent of a personal Messiah. Prayers in these liberal prayer books are presented in Hebrew and either translated or paraphrased in the vernacular. Some prayers appear only in translation. In spite of those differences, the basic rubric of the liturgy remains intact.

Most Jewish prayers are composed for the group rather than the individual. In many synagogues a quorum of ten men, called a *minyan,* is required for congregational worship. The synagogue is the preferred location for worship, but Jews may gather wherever a congregation is present. One may even pray alone, if necessary, at home, in an open field or on a journey. In every case, however, the language of prayer follows the plural form, such as ''our God'' and "our salvation," emphasizing the centrality of the prayer book as a source of unity for all Jews.

Jewish worship in more traditional circles also includes special attire. Orthodox and Conservative male Jews will never pray with uncovered heads. Many of them wear a *kipah* ("cap") not only during prayer but every hour of every waking day and night. For Sabbath and festival worship, it is also customary among many male Jews to wear a *tallith* ("prayer shawl"). The most pious among them will wear a special undergarment called a *tallith katan* which has fringes on all four corners as does the prayer shawl. The four-cornered garment is a vestige of the robe that was worn in ancient times and which still is worn among Bedouin tribesmen. The fringes attached to the corners serve religiously as a constant reminder to remain within the limits of decency, morality, and justice. The tallith is the forerunner to the pulpit stole in Christian worship.

Additional attire for the weekday morning service among the most observant Jewish men consists of a pair of phylacteries, known as *t'fillin,* which are attached to the forehead and the left arm. Each strap of the phylactery is attached to a small black box which contains a small parchment inscribed with words about the love of God. That which is worn on the arm is a symbol of the duty to act in observance of the Covenant. The phylactery worn on the forehead serves to remind the wearer of his duty to think continually of God's commandments. T'fillin are worn every morning except on Shabbat; because the Sabbath is the supreme sign of the Covenant, no other reminder is required.

Reform Judaism many years ago discontinued the use of the tallith and t'fillin, although a number of congregations have recently restored the practice of wearing kipah and tallith on an optional basis. Very few Reform Jews maintain the custom of wearing t'fillin.

Judaism teaches that God responds to prayer, but carefully delineates the conditions and limits of prayer. One cannot rely on words alone to achieve the purpose of prayer. Prayer is at best an incentive, a catalyst for action. It is not in any way a secret formula for ensuring a favorable outcome for personal requests of various kinds. A Jewish approach would encourage one to pray as if everything depended on God but to act as if everything depended on the individual.

If a person is ill, it is not sufficient simply to pray to God for recovery. A thoughtful Jew will also count on his physician as well as his Creator. Otherwise he abuses his own soul and discredits God, who endowed specialists in medicine with the skill and knowledge to restore their patients to good health.

Most religious Jews nowadays will agree that prayer is an exceedingly potent mechanism for articulating human fears and apprehensions, for clarifying vague and obscure thoughts, for mobilizing courage and determination, and for maintaining emotional strength and stability. Most will also agree that prayer can unlock enormous depths of human potential and inspire a level of performance totally beyond any ordinary expectation.

At the same time Jews will differ considerably in their explanations for the power of prayer. Some attribute the phenomenon to purely naturalistic causes, even though this view may be foreign to the tradition. The impact of prayer for them is the result of the human psyche responding to the idea of a reality as awesome as that of divine judgment. The individual, in this view, is ultimately the source of his own inspiration.

The vast majority of religious Jews, however, will appeal to more traditional theological explanations. Prayer for them is an experience which completely overwhelms an individual with the divine presence. The encounter is not subject to the ordinary dictates of reason, and therefore, it is impossible for naturalistic law to illuminate it.

The advocates of a more naturalistic faith would insist that prayer must function within a natural law as science defines it and that reasonable people can expect nothing more than that. The conventional majority, on the other hand, contends that natural law is not absolute but is itself a creation of divine intelligence and therefore subject to divine control. Nothing in this context is impossible, including the occurrence of miracles.

DAILY OBSERVANCE

An adequate understanding of the role of ritual mitzvot in the daily life of an observant Jew requires an insight into the routine of an ordinary day in his life. From the moment he awakens until the time he retires, a Jew fills his day with words of gratitude to his Maker. He recites a blessing for washing his hands and face, for setting foot on the floor, for attending to his bodily needs, and for dressing in his customary garments. Women are exempted from these obligations, in part because Judaism originated in a patriarchal Oriental culture, but also in large measure because the sages deliberately excused women as homemakers from all positive commandments in which time was considered a determining factor.

After completing these early morning rituals, male Jews then continue with their morning worship, including tallith and t'fillin, together with all the appropriate benedictions. In the company of a congregation with a minyan (minimal quorum of ten men), that service might require as much as an hour to conduct.

The most observant Jews do not taste any food before this service is over. Even then the daily regimen provides for the ritual of washing hands and a brief prayer of thankfulness before the meal begins with the blessing over bread. Following the meal, a series of benedictions is chanted. According to the sages, these are even more commendable than the earlier grace. They explain that distinction by observing that it requires much less incentive to thank God for food when one is hungry before a meal than when one is satisfied afterwards.

A formal worship service will follow twice more during the day, once in the afternoon and again in the evening. In between those times, a Jew may invoke God's name repeatedly, because benedictions are assigned to almost every conceivable experience, such as eating between meals, sitting down to study Torah, purchasing and wearing a new garment, beginning a journey, tasting a new fruit of the season, seeing lightning, hearing thunder, watching the ocean, observing a rainbow, or noticing trees beginning to blossom in spring. A blessing exists even for meeting a person who is learned in Torah or general studies, for hearing good news or absorbing bad news. In addition, every person is expected to devote a portion of each day to the study of his heritage, either privately or as a student in a class.

Finally, before a male Jew retires, he prays once more in gratitude for rest and refreshment of soul. One might easily conclude that days filled with such an abundance of ritual would leave little time for work or other activities. The truth is that much less time is absorbed with these matters than most people would suppose, because almost all of them may be executed simultaneously with the actions they sanctify and demand very little additional time. In any event, the Jews who follow this schedule are not deterred by the measure of time it absorbs. For them the major themes of human existence are God and the good life, and addressing those priorities far surpasses any other considerations.

Because it was the realm of daily activity which distinguished the Jewish community for centuries, a description of Jewish dietary laws deserves special recognition. Jewish tradition generally classified these laws under the generic term of *kashruth* (''ritual fitness''). Kashruth technically refers not only to properly prepared foods but to ritual objects of any kind. A Torah scroll may or may not be *kosher* (''ritually fit'') depending upon its composition and its condition. The same principle applies to a tallith, a *ner tamid* (the eternal light on the altar in the synagogue) or a *mezuzah* (a small encased scroll attached to the ''doorpost'' of a Jewish home).

In its application to food, kashruth is based upon biblical injunctions about prohibited foods which are detailed in Leviticus 11 and Deuteronomy 14. All vegetables and fruits are permitted. In other categories, prohibited meats include the flesh of all animals such as horses and pigs, whose hooves are not cloven and which do not chew the cud. Only fish with fins and scales are permitted, which, therefore, excludes all shellfish. Fowl which are unclean because they are birds of prey are not kosher.

Even ritually permissible foods must be slaughtered in a carefully prescribed manner by a person who is licensed for that purpose and is known as a *shochet* (''ritual slaughterer''). Carcasses of kosher animals may not reveal any trace of serious disease, especially in the lungs. They must also be drained of blood; this is accomplished by the slaughtering method and by soaking and salting the meat before it is cooked.

Furthermore, meat and meat products may not be prepared, served, or eaten with milk products or milk derivatives. Utensils and dishes that belong to one category may not be mixed with those of the other. A person must even wait a specified period of time between consuming portions of meat and milk products.

Whatever is forbidden according to the categories of kashruth is termed *terefah,* which in Hebrew means literally "torn" and referred originally to any living animal that had fallen victim to a beast or bird of prey and was therefore unacceptable as a food. Eventually, the concept of terefah extended to all forbidden foods.

Much has been spoken and written about the origin and purpose of dietary laws. More than ample evidence exists to trace their roots to tribal taboos long before the emergence of the Jewish people. Other sources justify them as early examples of public health laws. Both hypotheses contain an element of truth. Although modern scholarship discredits the theory, many provisions of kashruth may reflect an appreciation for sanitation and cleanliness. Jews always insisted on purity in the preparation of food and food inspection. Such requirements were based on religious conviction but also ensured a high level of public health. The prohibition of shellfish, especially in a warm climate such as Palestine where spoilage was a constant danger, was unusually sound and sensible.

The observant Jew, however, attached a radically different meaning to these dietary laws based on three considerations. First, and most important, the dietary laws were elevated to the category of divine laws. Their ultimate purpose was known to God, if not to mortal man. Their observance was evidence of obedience to God's will, a recognition of His supreme authority. If God has willed them, His servants must obey them. The observance of dietary laws was a discipline in holiness.

Secondly, for Jews who observed them, dietary laws were a means of preserving the uniqueness of the Jewish people. Their observance was a bond which the Jews could share only with each other and which therefore diminished the prospect of assimilating into the surrounding culture. People who cannot eat with strangers are not likely to live with them.

Finally, kashruth provided the Jewish community with a symbolic act which stressed the reverence for group identity. It served a purpose similar to the ceremonial procedures of various fraternal orders which activate and reinforce the attachments of members to their principles, their history, and tradition. Kashruth was the emblem of the Jewish people. It served as a constant reminder to every individual Jew of his responsibilities to Judaism and other Jews.

The observance of dietary laws today ranges from complete adherence to complete abstention. A number of Jews reject the claim of divine origin for such laws, while others insist that considerations of public health and nutrition may have applied in ancient times but no longer do.

Other Jews reject the notion of divine revelation, but still defend the observance of kashruth as part of a timeless pattern of respect for enduring standards in Jewish life. Dietary laws thus deserve the same regard as customs in a foreign country for visitors or conventional manners in a particular social setting.

Still other Jews will observe kashruth at home but not outside. Some are even selective about home observance, maintaining part but not all of the dietary requirements. Many will simply deny themselves specific foods, such as pork or shellfish, as a matter of religious discipline or from personal dislike.

At the same time there are a great many Jews who obey the laws of kashruth without compromise and who are pleased and proud to do so. For them the adjustments and accommodations which kashruth requires are insignificant and pose no serious hardship. The distance that separates them in this regard from the total society is not easily ignored, but obedience to God and faith in His commandments more than merit the sacrifice of that inconvenience.

In any event, observance of kashruth is not always a barometer of devotion to Judaism and the Covenant. Many of the most serious Jews—serious in terms of their commitment to the most sacred ideals of Jewish faith—may eat shrimp with an untroubled conscience, while their Jewish neighbors may know little and care less about the spiritual imperatives of Judaism but eat only kosher food out of sheer force of habit. Kashruth is a significant indicator of Jewish piety, but not always as reliable as its advocates sometimes imply.

FROM BIRTH TO DEATH

The appeal of religion generally derived from its power to sanctify climactic moments in human experience from birth to death. The Covenant is such an instrument for elevating the milestones of an individual's life to a level of divine significance. In terms of the Covenant, those events compromise that pattern of observances called the life cycle.

Much of life is sameness and repetition. Parts of it, however, are unique. They include occasions that occur only once, never to return. The Covenant in Judaism prescribes an appropriate response to every critical juncture in a person's journey through this world.

That response begins with birth and the naming of newborn children. If the baby is a boy, he is welcomed into the Jewish community through the ceremony of *b'rith milah,* the "covenant of circumcision." Circumcision began with Abraham (Gen. 17:10–27) as the seal of the Covenant between him and God. It transformed Abraham into a Jew. Ever since that time, all male children were bound by the same ritual. Although anthropologists may cite primitive origins for this practice and modern medicine may acclaim its hygienic value, the observant Jew has kept it as a sign of his conviction that his Covenant with God is irrevocably linked literally to his physical survival.

Circumcision is performed by a *mohel,* a specialist for this purpose, wherever and whenever possible. Being a mohel is an honor and a great distinction, because officiating at a b'rith milah is a privilege and a cherished mitzvah.

In earlier times circumcision was often performed in the synagogue. Although it is still performed there occasionally, nowadays the usual location is either the hospital or the home. Traditional custom requires the presence of a minyan (the minimum quorum of ten men) for this ceremony.

Two chairs are placed in front of the mohel. One of them is reserved for a relative, usually a grandfather or uncle, whose privilege it is to hold the child during the procedure and who then becomes the child's godfather. The other chair is left unoccupied as the symbolic place for Elijah the prophet, who is enshrined in Jewish legend as the guardian of Israel's eternal Covenant with God.

When the child is brought in for the ceremony, the mohel recites a prayer seeking God's assistance and continues with a blessing for the act of circumcision itself. The father of the child also adds a benediction in presenting his son for entry into the Covenant of Abraham.

By the time the father has completed his prayer, the mohel has usually performed the surgery and responds by leading the guests in declaring, "As he has entered the Covenant, so may he come to enter the realm of Torah, of marriage, and of good deeds."

Finally, the joy of the occasion is sanctified with the blessing over wine. The wine cup used for the b'rit milah is then set aside as a special family possession to be used again on other festive occasions in the boy's life, including his wedding.

If a mohel is unavailable for this ceremony, a Jewish physician will often perform the operation with a rabbi officiating over the religious ritual. In any case, the Torah forbids the observance of b'rit milah before the eighth day. Unfortunately, many hospitals nowadays automatically schedule male infants for circumcision on the third day or whenever it is convenient. Jewish law permits postponement of the ritual beyond the eighth day in extenuating circumstances, but under no conditions by traditional standards can the ceremony be justified before. Every effort should be made to ensure the observance of b'rit milah on the eighth day.

Just as male infants were named at their circumcision, female children were named in the synagogue. There the ceremony usually included an *aliyah* ("calling up") to the Torah for the father of the child during which time he would offer a special blessing for his wife and baby. The name of the child would then be mentioned in a petition to God to bless and protect her.

Several Reform congregations have recently expanded this naming ceremony into a *b'rit chayim,* a "covenant of life" ritual, to parallel the b'rit milah for boys. Very often that ceremony is observed at home in similar fashion to the ritual of circumcision. Most Reform congregations have also followed a custom in recent years of naming male children as well as female children in the synagogue on a Sabbath shortly after the infant's birth; at that time both parents are called to the pulpit in the presence of the congregation for a brief ceremony with the rabbi.

According to ancient Torah tradition, all first fruits and first children belonged to God. That legacy continued with the promise of Hannah (I Sam. 1:11) to dedicate the life of her future son to the service of the Temple if only she could conceive a child; thus all first-born male children in Jewish households are destined for duties of priesthood. In order to release a boy from this obligation, he must be redeemed by a contribution to the Temple. The ceremony for this purpose is called a *pidyon haben,* the "redemption of the firstborn." Since there is no longer either a Temple in Jerusalem or a priesthood in Judaism, the practice is largely meaningless in modern times. Nonetheless, some Jews continue to maintain it as a vestige of their ties to the past.

As a child grows to adolescence, he or she assumes increasingly larger responsibilities. The Mishnah teaches: "At five years the age is reached for the study of the Scriptures; at ten for the study of the Mishnah; at thirteen for the fulfillment of the commandments" (*Pirke Avot* 5:24).

In Talmudic times a father was responsible for his son's education up to the age of thirteen. The prevailing assumption was that a child had developed by that time at least a basic knowledge of Jewish life as it was presented in the classic texts of Judaism. After the age of thirteen, a young man did not abandon his studies; they simply became his own responsibility and no longer that of his parents.

The thirteenth year, then, was a significant milestone in the life of every young Jewish boy. To celebrate the completion of his total reliance on others for his moral and intellectual growth, and the beginning of his own accountability in that enterprise, he was called to recite the blessings over the Torah on the Sabbath immediately following his thirteenth birthday. At the same time, his father would declare, "Blessed be He who has freed me from responsibility for this child."

Sometime in the Middle Ages the custom evolved of designating a young man at this stage of life as a *bar mitzvah,* meaning literally, "a son of the commandment," but more freely signifying "a responsible Jew."

The paradox of modern American Jewish life is that even though parental supervision of a child's education extends far beyond the age of thirteen, the ceremony of bar mitzvah has expanded in significance rather than contracted. Enormous time, energy, and resources are devoted to preparation for bar mitzvah. Many Jewish religious schools concentrate their efforts on the bar mitzvah program and curriculum. Family and friends from every direction attend the Sabbath service for the ceremony.

The extent and nature of a youngster's participation varies from one synagogue to another. In many synagogues he may conduct a portion of the worship service or all of it. At the very least, he will be called to the pulpit to recite or chant the blessings for the Torah and to read a brief passage himself. In addition, he will deliver the haftarah and its blessings for that Shabbat. Usually, he will also prepare a talk for the congregation on the message of the Torah reading or on the requirements of adult Jewish living. Toward the conclusion of the service, the rabbi will invoke God's blessing on the young man and convey the best wishes of the congregation.

Invariably, the bar mitzvah ceremony is followed by a joyous social celebration. The family will often serve refreshments to the entire congregation after the Sabbath service. Family and friends may then continue with a larger reception at home or in a public facility. The bar mitzvah boy is frequently flooded with gifts and contributions in his honor, and on occasion will acknowledge his gratitude with a donation of his own to a worthy cause.

More recently, in Conservative and Reform Judaism especially, this ritual also includes girls. In most cases, the ceremony is exactly the same or very similar, except that for girls it is called a *bat mitzvah,* meaning "a daughter of the commandment."

The ceremony of confirmation, which was discussed earlier with reference to the festival of Shavuoth, is a life cycle observance for boys and girls completing the formal program of religious education at the age of fifteen or sixteen. Nearly all Reform synagogues have adopted this practice, as have many Conservative and even several Orthodox synagogues, even though the Reform movement was severely criticized for adapting this practice from non-Jewish sources. Whereas bar and bat mitzvah ceremonies focus on each child individually, confirmation is a collective group experience which emphasizes the mutual obligations of all the Jewish people in fulfilling the terms of the Covenant. It is a way of articulating loyalty to Judaism either through a creative worship service, brief messages, a cantata, dance, audio-visual experience, or any other creative vehicle of spiritual expression. It is the culmination of the total religious school program for those synagogues which observe it.

Marriage in Judaism is a wholesome fulfillment, a sacred bond, an intrinsic good. It is, in terms of the Covenant, a supreme paradigm of a mitzvah. In Jewish mysticism, "He who has no wife is not a man, for Scripture teaches that God created them male and female, and called *their* name Adam" (*Zohar, Genesis* 55b). The Talmud declares that "he who remains unmarried impairs the divine image'' (*Yebamoth* 63b), and that ''one who does not marry dwells without joy, without blessing, without goodness, . . . without peace'' (*Yebamoth* 62b). According to Talmudic law, the High Priest was not permitted to perform the atonement rituals of Yom Kippur unless he was married.

Perhaps one of the most exalted and most tender affirmations of marriage is the passage from the Midrash (*Genesis Rabbah* 68:4) in which a Roman matron asked Rabbi Jose, '''In how many days did you say your God created His world?'

'In six days,' replied Rabbi Jose.

'If that's the case,' continued the Roman matron, 'what has He been doing ever since?'

Rabbi Jose explained, 'He has been sitting at His throne and making matches, assigning this man to that woman, this woman to that man, and so on.'''

Actually, Rabbi Jose's response was only a reaffirmation of an earlier statement in the Midrash that ''no man should be without a wife, nor a woman without a husband, nor both of them without God'' (*Kiddushin* 30b).

Marriage in Judaism, then, is a divine commandment, because it is a vehicle for human spiritual fulfillment. It provides a conducive setting in which a person can best demonstrate a capacity to live beyond one's self out of love and consideration for another human being. Lasting affection and concern for another person could not be left to spontaneous impulse or momentary whim. It required a constant conditioning and adjustment. Ordinary marital responsibilities, so distasteful and pedestrian to much of modern society, were by no means burdens in Jewish tradition. They were instead the anvils on which husband and wife forged bonds of patience, determination, and perseverance that would sustain them in their difficulties as well as in their happiness.

The ideal in Judaism centered not on the idea of separating oneself from others, but of transcending oneself so that the ''I'' encompassed the marriage partner in mutual love and esteem. Marriage was a major step toward maturity in the life-long process of expanding the limits of mind and heart. When the sages designated God as a partner to every marriage, they meant that the marital bond was sanctioned by divine authority, that both spouses were responsible to God for their decisions, and that husband and wife could not become tools or means for one another in achieving selfish ends. The Talmud observes in this context: "As husband and wife are worthy, God's glory dwells in their midst" (*Sota* 17a).

The rabbinic sages certainly never heard of the women's movement and surely would never have endorsed it if they had. No traditional Oriental religion, including Judaism, ever elevated women to complete equality with men. Oriental cultures, out of which Judaism and Christianity emerged, were patterned after a patriarchal model of society. The eldest male of the family or tribe exercised final and supreme authority. The history of ancient Israel and its sister civilizations is a story determined and dominated largely by men.

Nevertheless, in its provisions for marriage, Judaism achieved a unique distinction in contrast to all non-Jewish cultures. It attempted to establish by law a mutually acceptable arrangement that does not violate the integrity of either partner. That attempt expressed itself in a variety of legal conditions.

In the first place, Judaism teaches that marriage is valid only by mutual consent. Throughout the Middle Ages, when parents frequently arranged matches for their children, Jewish law ordained that it was forbidden for a man to betroth his minor daughter. Even when she had attained her majority her father could not arrange her marriage unless she said of the proposed fiancé, "I love this man." The law further stipulated that the groom could not even enter the bridal chamber to consummate the marriage without the bride's permission.

With regard to matters of intimacy between husband and wife, it is most instructive to understand the approach of Jewish tradition to the nature of sexual relations. Sexuality in Judaism was almost always considered to be a necessary and healthy function of human personality. Sex was not sinful or shameful. A certain prudishness prevailed periodically in Jewish communities, but usually Jews exhibited an exceptionally open and honest approach to sexual morality. While a debate still rages in many places about the wisdom of sex education in public schools, Jewish students of the Talmud covered such topics as puberty, conception, menstruation, birth control, and breast feeding by the time they were eleven or twelve years of age. The subject of sex was not obscene.

These students therefore were not shocked, as some modern readers might be, to learn that Jewish law provided that husband and wife should not have sexual intercourse while either is intoxicated, sluggish or in mourning, nor when the wife is asleep, nor if the husband overpowers her, but only with the consent and happy disposition of both. The sexual act in Judaism is the culmination of a loving relationship in which both partners find and share mutual satisfaction. It does not exist only for the purpose of producing children. To the contrary, the sages submitted that the beauty, character, and health of the offspring were often influenced by the nature of the sexual relations. More than that, sexual relations were not to cease after a woman's menopause. A man satisfied his conjugal obligation even if his wife were sterile or if she suffered from a disability which made conception impossible.

One of the worst obscenities was cohabitation without the spiritual components of love and consideration for one another. In Jewish mysticism "the bond between male and female is the secret of true faith" (*Zohar Genesis* 101b).

Jewish law specifically provided that a wife should use cosmetics and wear ornaments that would make her attractive to her husband not only in her youth but also in her old age. One of the leading authorities of medieval Jewry added: "Let a curse descend upon a woman who has a husband and does not strive to be attractive" (Meir of Rothenberg, *Responsa* #199).

On the matter of birth control, Judaism was far in the vanguard of the current moral climate. If a woman's life was in danger, or if the health of the child was in jeopardy, or if there were negative hereditary or environmental factors, the rabbis not only permitted, but in some cases required, methods of contraception. Never, however, did they advocate total abstention. Procreation was most assuredly a serious responsibility in marriage, but love and companionship were at least as important in Jewish tradition. The sages reminded their students that Eve was created to be a "helper" to Adam, since, in the words of God himself, "It is not good that the man should be alone. . . ." (Gen. 2:18). Only later on, after they had known and loved each other, did God command them both to "be fruitful and multiply. . . ." (Gen. 1:28).

The dominant tendency in Judaism was an attempt to establish a single standard of conduct for husband and wife and to strive for equality between both partners. This is the major consideration which shaped attitudes toward polygamy, divorce, and relations between bride and groom.

These reciprocal responsibilities affected every facet of the marital arrangement. Rabbinic law required a husband to provide his wife with food, shelter, ornaments, and pocket money in accordance with his means, and, so far as he was able, to the level to which she was accustomed. The general principle stipulates that "the wife ascends with her husband, but does not descend with him" (see *Genesis Rabbah* 17.2 and *Ketuboth* 11.3). She was entitled to all the advantages of his status without losing those she enjoyed in her parents' home. At the same time, since a husband was obliged to provide for his wife's sustenance, he had a claim on all her personal earnings.

On the subject of divorce, a woman was entitled to dissolve the marriage if it took place under false pretenses, if the husband was immoral, if his profession was intolerable to her, if they were sexually incompatible, if he embarrassed her, denied her entry to their home, if his demands blemished her reputation, if he angered easily, insulted her, beat her, or left her for an unreasonable length of time.

A husband could file for divorce for no less serious grounds and, in some cases, for even more trivial ones. Some authorities would permit a divorce if a man found another woman more attractive than his wife (*Mishnah, Gitten* 9.10). In some instances a wife might sue for divorce, and the husband could refuse to grant it. A religious court might occasionally compel the husband to yield, but not always. Whatever the grounds for divorce might have been, Jewish law required a *bet din* (a "rabbinic court") to issue a religious bill of divorce. This requirement still applies in Orthodox and Conservative Judaism, in addition to any civil document for such purpose.

However lenient provisions might have been for divorce, the Jewish community always exerted enormous moral and social pressure against it. Divorce was consequently a rare phenomenon in Jewish life. The Talmud observed: "The altar sheds tears over him who divorces his first wife . . . because the Lord grieves over such separation" (*Gittin* 90b). Nevertheless, Judaism recognized that the sanctity of a marriage dissolves when both partners no longer love or care for each other. To punish both of them by compelling them to remain together would make a mockery of all that such a union should and does imply—understanding, patience, mutual respect, and consideration for the life of someone very precious.

Marriage in Judaism is not a sacrament beyond the authority of any human agency. There are no sacraments at all in Judaism. Marriage is called *kiddushin*—a word that derives from the Hebrew term meaning "holy." Marriage is something holy, but the word for "holy" in Hebrew means more specifically "to separate." When a man and a woman marry, they separate themselves from all others in order to make their life together something distinctive and precious. That is what we mean by *"holy"*—making something special and different, whether it be the Sabbath, holiday festivals, or joyous occasions of any kind, including most assuredly the magnificent mystery of love between husband and wife.

The traditional Jewish wedding ceremony is the ritual embodiment of all these aspirations. It begins with a statement of welcome to the bride and groom. It continues with blessings over two goblets of wine. The first is a vestige of the ancient *erusin* ("engagement") ceremony. Until the eleventh or twelfth century this portion of the ceremony was completed separately several months before the actual wedding. The two cups of wine therefore symbolically link the two previously separated portions of the marriage service.

The groom proceeds by placing a plain gold ring upon the finger of the bride while he pronounces the formula in Hebrew and then in English: "Be thou consecrated unto me with this ring as my wife, according to the law of Moses and the faith of Israel."

The *k'tubah* ("marriage contract") is then read. In the Diaspora, this emphasizes the moral obligations of marriage as well as the legal conditions, since the legality of the marriage is usually defined by a civil marriage license.

Much of the purpose and significance of Jewish marriage is articulated in the recitation or chanting of the seven wedding benedictions. Toward the end of the ceremony, the bridegroom breaks a glass with his foot, symbolizing the destruction of Jerusalem in the first century of the Common Era, the most catastrophic event in Jewish history until the Holocaust of the twentieth century. That gesture fulfills a basic precept in Judaism: a reminder of sorrow must be included on every occasion of joy, just as a reminder of gladness must be included on every occasion of sadness. This observance reinforces the truth that human experience is rarely a matter of unmitigated bliss or disappointment, but usually a bittersweet blend of both.

The ceremony concludes with a kiss between bride and groom and shouts of *mazel tov* ("good luck") from the guests. The wedding celebration then begins.

Every traditional wedding is performed beneath a *chuppah* ("wedding canopy"). Usually this item consists of a large square piece of beautifully embroidered cloth material, supported by four poles that are either fixed to the floor or held by friends of the family. The chuppah is a symbol of the marital chamber or the home which the bride and groom are about to build. In Reform Jewish ceremonies, it is optional. So, too, are the *ketubah* and the second cup of wine.

Most important, the marriage ceremony itself is the most graphic and emphatic method of dramatizing the enduring principle that in Judaism God is a partner to every covenant between husband and wife. Rabbi Akiba taught: "If husband and wife are worthy, then God abides with them; if not, fire consumes them" (*Sota* 17a). The marriage bond is a divine blessing and should be treated with the sanctity it deserves. The home is a sanctuary, and husband and wife minister to its needs as the priests of old in the Temple at Jerusalem. For man and woman, marriage is part of the eternal covenant between God and the people of Israel.

Few subjects produce more distress than the subject of death and dying. That distress is readily understandable, because death embraces the realm of the unknown, and the unknown ranks among the most terrifying of all mortal fears. In some civilizations the dominating impulse consisted of denying the ultimate reality of death. Such societies usually assigned to religion the task of disguising the grim facts of death and attempted to convince themselves that dying was simply another step in the total life process.

Probably the best examples of such metaphysical camouflage were the pyramids of Egypt. The pyramid was actually a transitional shelter for the pharaoh in his passage from this world to another. He was buried with his weapons, his wealth, his material possessions, and sufficient food to sustain him on his journey to a new life in a new world. The American Indians followed similar procedures in their burial practices, and even Christianity and Islam developed elaborate theologies about heaven and hell and the nature of that other universe in which the dead shall live again.

Judaism did not escape this influence entirely, but it demonstrated vigorous resistance to such tendencies in the course of its historical development. The classical literature in Judaism contains lengthy discussions on the subject of death and its meaning; but it has resisted the urge, so common elsewhere, to make it a major concern or even to soften its grim reality.

Judaism has never developed a systematic concept of death and the world beyond. It embraces as many views on the subject as there are viewers. Matters of belief never intruded on the domain of Jewish law. The rabbinic sages always acted collectively on matters of religious observance, but never on religious belief. They dictated the number of times a Jew must recite the Shema each day, but never what it means.

Nonetheless, on subjects of a conceptual nature such as death and dying, it is possible to recognize certain emerging patterns and unifying themes, and it may be helpful to identify these themes for a clearer understanding of the actual practices associated with death and burial in Judaism.

One major theme is the inevitability of death. Judaism teaches that death is not an illusion but a reality—an awesome reality. It is the complete and final termination of life as we know it. It requires an irreversible separation between an individual and his family and friends. The perception of death is best reflected in the words of the wise woman of Tekoah who conceded, "We must all die, we are like water spilt on the ground, which cannot be gathered up again" (2 Sam. 14:14).

Man is under "the sentence of death," as it were. Still, that condition is not necessarily a calamity. Although the Psalmist declared that man is but "a wind that passes and comes not again" (Ps. 78:39), he also excluded boundless confidence in the outcome of the human enterprise when he inquired:

> Whither shall I go from Thy spirit?
> Or whither shall I flee from Thy presence?
> If I ascend to Heaven, Thou art there!

If I make my bed in Sheol [the netherworld],
  Thou art there!
If I take the wings of the morning and dwell
  in the uttermost parts of the sea,
Even there Thy hand shall lead me, and Thy
  right hand shall hold me.
And if I say, "Let only darkness cover
  me, and the light about me be night,"
even the darkness is not dark to Thee,
the night is bright as the day;
  for darkness is as light with Thee."

[Ps. 139:7–12]

Death is real and inevitable. But in the presence of death, man often learns to understand better the meaning of life.

A second major theme of death in Jewish thought is the affirmation of life. Rabbinic literature teaches: "Better is one day of happiness and good deeds in this world than all the life in the world to come" (*Mishna, Avot* 4:22). Judaism dwells far more on love of life than fear of death. Life offers man his only opportunity to prove he can be a partner with God in creating a better world. The word or a toast in Jewish circles is not "cheers" or "bottoms up," but *"l'chayim"*—"to life." Stated simply, while Judaism does not ignore the mystery of death, it is concerned primarily with the miracle of life.

The inevitability of death and the affirmation of life shaped a Jew's attitude toward human existence; but those attitudes did not preclude some speculation about the nature and destiny of the soul. One such concept was the notion of *t'chiat hametim,* the "resurrection of the dead."

The belief in the resurrection of Jesus in early Christianity traced its theological roots to Jewish soil. The most visible evidence for that claim is in the statements of the apostle Paul about bodily resurrection to predominantly Jewish audiences. When he spoke to the Gentiles, he alluded only to a nonphysical, spiritual immortality which was popular among the Greek mystery cults and other religious sects in the Mediterranean world. In Orthodox Jewish thought to the present day, the belief continues that the dead will rise bodily and be judged by God at the end of time to determine whether or not they will share in the blessings of the Messianic Age.

More important, however, than any statements of beliefs or concepts surrounding death are actual observances. Among all ancient Jewish communal organizations, one of the most highly respected and admired was the *chevra kadishah* ("holy society"). The chevra kadishah consisted of men and women of superior religious merit who facilitated the care of the dying and the dead. Tradition bestowed the highest acclaim on their labor, because their motives for helping those who could never reciprocate could never be impugned.

As a person approached death, members of the chevra kadishah would rotate in keeping the person company. They would offer prayers, recite psalms, or listen in strict confidence to the individual's confession of sin before death. If a person could summon sufficient strength, the society member would even recite the Shema with him or her as the last mitzvah for any Jew in the final moment among humankind.

Jewish law forbids any effort either to hasten or delay the onset of death. To be certain that life had terminated, at a time when more sophisticated means were unavailable, a feather was placed on the body's lips for evidence that breathing had completely ceased.

In the preparation of the body for burial and in the observance of mourning customs, simplicity is the cornerstone of modern Jewish practice. The coffin, to be made entirely of wood, is deliberately plain and unpretentious to emphasize the equality in death of rich and poor alike. The body is thoroughly washed and cleansed and dressed in the traditional white shroud with utmost care and tenderness. A tallit is also draped around a man's shoulders. The most traditional Jews still forbid the practice of embalming, which violates the injunction of permitting the body to return promptly to the dust from which it came.

A Jewish funeral follows the moment of death as soon as possible. *Halakah* (Jewish law) stipulates that burial should take place within twenty-four hours after one has died. It also allows, however, for a minimal delay for the purpose of honoring the dead with the presence of family and friends who must travel long distances to show their reverence. Funerals may not be conducted on the Sabbath, in keeping with the precept that joy must always supersede sorrow, but they may be held on the intermediary days of major festivals.

In traditional practice, family and friends follow the coffin in procession to the cemetery. Before the service commences, the mourners tear their garment on the left side if the deceased is a parent and on the right side if any other relative, while they recite the benediction that concludes with blessing God as "the righteous Judge."

The funeral service consists essentially of several psalms interspersed with appropriate prayers and benedictions. A *hesped* ("eulogy") is delivered in praise of the individual's outstanding attributes and with consideration of comfort for the bereaved. The service concludes with the recitation of the *Kaddish*, the sanctification of God's name, which is a doxology glorifying the goodness of God even in the midst of deepest sorrow and grief. The kaddish is not a prayer for the dead, but a supreme statement of trust and confidence in the divine order of existence.

The initial period of mourning called *shivah* ("seven") is observed in traditional practice for seven days following the time of burial. In Reform Judaism it may be limited to three days based upon a consideration in Jewish law which permits such an abbreviated term (*Moed Katan* 15b). A person is forbidden during this period to perform any work that is not absolutely necessary. All energy and activity is directed to thoughts of the deceased. Shivah is required of every individual upon the death of a parent, child, sibling, or spouse. It is a difficult period, but it serves most effectively to keep the bereaved from brooding excessively over their loss, to keep them mentally alert and absorbed with the needs of the living. The steady stream of condolence calls helps to soften the agony of death in the knowledge that family and friends share some measure of the grief and sorrow that has occurred.

After shivah concludes, the period of *shloshim* ("thirty") continues from the date of burial. Traditionally, during this span of thirty days the mourners resume their ordinary routines but continue to recite certain prayers and to exercise discretion in their public conduct. At the end of shloshim, the formal period of mourning usually terminates except for the regular recitation of daily kaddish for eleven months.

Unfortunately, the demands and temptations of modern living have altered many of these customary practices. Regrettably, their neglect often complicates and prolongs the recovery of mourners from the pain of death and separation. People are often the saddest victims of their own disregard for tradition.

Jewish mourning customs are especially significant because they are community rituals. They are performed by those who share an identical religious attachment. They provide a reassurance and emotional bond which Freud once called "the clear awareness of an inner identity, the secret of the same inner construction." The collective rituals produce a feeling of solidarity or belonging and the certainty that one is a member of a distinctive group with all the comfort, gratification, pride, and even pain that such feelings encompass. The ceremony is the same for all. It is definite and explicit. Everyone knows that if he or she fulfills the requirements, no one could do more.

Jewish tradition is careful to limit the mourning period to specific practices within a definite timetable. It deliberately discourages excessive grief. Embittered sorrow is a sign of insufficient trust in God. No one can ever be the same after bereavement as before, but one is expected to resume a normal existence for the sake of life itself. It is interesting to note that Jewish law permits a mourner to sew together and wear again the garment that had been torn as a sign of grief. The explanation is that a scar may remain in the heart as on the garment, but life resumes its course.

Both in principle and in practice, the response to death in Judaism is much like a journey from the valley of despair to the higher road of affirmative, positive living. The Jewish response is an attempt to confront the naked reality of life, to give honor to the dead, but to guide the bereaved toward a new appreciation and fresh enthusiasm for the miracle of human existence. The Jew looks not beyond this world, but directly into it, and seeks by his labor to leave it a little better than he found it.

4
Israel: The People

Arise, shine; for your light has come,
and the glory of the Lord has risen upon you.
For behold, darkness shall cover the earth,
and thick darkness the peoples;
but the Lord will arise upon you,
and His glory will be seen upon you.
And nations shall come to your light,
and kings to the brightness of your rising.

Isa. 60:1-3

THE JEWISH PEOPLE AND THEIR NEIGHBORS

In terms of supporting and perpetuating the Covenant, Judaism assigns equal responsibility to both parties, only one of whom is the author of that Covenant, God. The other is the people of Israel whom God has separated from all others to labor for Him and with Him in completing the endless task of creation. Both are partners in that enterprise. Israel's dependence on God is self-evident, but God's dependence upon Israel is crucial though less obvious.

One of the sages inquired what God might have meant by the scriptural verse, "For I have spread you abroad as the four winds of the heavens" (Zech. 2:6). He emphasized that the verse reads "as the four winds" rather than "upon the four winds," which implies that the four winds were not a device for dispersing Israel, but that, just as no place in the world is without wind, so also the world cannot exist without the people of Israel (*Taanith* 3b). The Jewish people are the instrument or catalyst for activating the conscience of all mankind in the service of God. The Covenant is the formula for initiating and sustaining that process.

Whatever differences may separate the Jewish people in assessing their responsibilities to God in these matters, they are keenly aware of their responsibility to each other. The unity of the Jewish people is almost a categorical imperative. The Talmud declares: "All Jews are bondsmen one for another" (*Shebuot* 39a), and elsewhere, "All people are responsible for each other" (*Sanhedrin* 27b). However a Jew may qualify his or her religious attachments, membership in and loyalty to the Jewish people are nonnegotiable requirements.

Judaism teaches that membership in the Jewish people may derive either from birth or conversion (or, as some have recently observed, "by chance or by choice"). According to Jewish law, a person may be a Jew by birth only if the mother is Jewish. Reform practice, contrary to Orthodox and Conservative practice, has expanded that provision to include either parent, so long as a family demonstrates evidence of raising their children in the Jewish faith. In any case, a Jew by birth can never be deprived of Jewish identity. He or she may dissociate himself or herself entirely from Judaism, but he or she will still remain a member of the Jewish people.

The term *convert* is not the best word to describe an individual who has decided to become a Jew by choice. Convert and conversion derive from the Latin root *convertere,* meaning to turn or change from one state to another. Judaism does not require such a transformation. Rather, it encourages a process of welcoming a person into the peoplehood of Israel, the family of Jews. In Hebrew, the proper terminology is *ger* ("male") or *gioret* ("female") with reference to proselytes. The Hebrew words mean "stranger" and have evolved into a broader category of "righteous individuals" who, after acquiring knowledge of Judaism and experience in Jewish living, proclaim that they want to be Jews and agree to be part of the Jewish people under all conditions.

Jewish law requires circumcision of all males who become Jews and *mikveh* (ritual immersion in water) of both men and women who choose Judaism. These procedures are mandatory in Orthodox and Conservative Judaism, but not in Reform Judaism. In any case, Halakah stipulates that a Jew by choice who satisfies the requirements of conversion occupies exactly the same rank and status as a Jew by birth. They are all part of *k'lal yisrael* (the "total community of Israel").

In more recent times the solidarity of the Jewish people has expressed itself in terms of *am'cha* ("peoplehood"). Jews speak of commitment and loyalty to one another as am'cha. Am'cha is the attachment that transcends all diversity. It is the all-inclusive common denominator of Jewish unity. It refers to a sense of extended family kinship which encourages unconditional support and trust between people who may be strangers to each other except for their Jewish ties. Like members of a family, Jews react to their experience collectively. When one hurts, all hurt; when one suffers, all suffer.

It is not a matter of being any more blind to the faults or shortcomings of the total community than to those of parents or children, brothers or sisters. One does not ignore their poor judgment, but their failures are no more reason for rejecting them than their success is for accepting them. All family members belong to each other and always will regardless of differences or imperfections.

Jews are like a family because they believe in and need one another. Family attachments are almost unconditional. Mutual encouragement and reassurance are the building blocks of confidence in the total effort.

To be sure, not every Jew is a model of such supreme loyalty to his people, but neither is every member of an ordinary family. The behavior which most members exhibit, however, demonstrates the primary attachment of brothers and sisters for each other in contrast to others.

Since the middle of the twentieth century, it has been impossible to appreciate the centrality of Jewish peoplehood as a component of the Covenant without understanding the meaning of the most catastrophic event in all Jewish experience. The worst calamity Jews ever suffered was the deliberate extermination of more than six million of their people by the Nazis before and during World War II (1933–45).

That mindless slaughter is usually described as the *Holocaust,* "a burnt offering completely consumed by fire." In Hebrew, the word is *olah,* implying a necessary sacrifice for the purpose of seeking atonement or divine forgiveness for some transgression. Israelis call the Holocaust the *ṣhoah,* which refers to a total destruction or devastation.

More recently another suggestion for conveying the enormity of the massacre of more than one-third of world Jewry is the term *churban*. This word also means "destruction"; but unlike holocaust or shoah, churban relates to a more specific Jewish historical context. The destruction of the First Temple in 586 B.C.E. and the Second Temple in 70 C.E. were both called churban. Surely, according to the supporters of this view, the destruction of European Jewry belongs in the same category for both its historical and theological implications.

For general historical purposes, the Holocaust encompasses the period from January 30, 1933, when Hitler became Chancellor of Germany, to May 8, 1945, when the Nazis surrendered. The term *Final Solution* refers to the Nazi plans to liquidate physically all the Jews of Europe. The term was introduced at the Wannsee Conference held in Berlin in early 1942 at which German military leaders ordered its implementation.

While thousands of Jews were murdered by the Nazis or died as a direct result of discriminatory measures instituted against Jews during the initial years of the Third Reich, the systematic murder of Jews did not begin until the German invasion of the Soviet Union in June 1941.

The first official measures against the Jews may be traced to September 1935 and the passage of the infamous Nuremberg Laws. Those laws legalized a boycott of Jewish shops and businesses and excluded from the civil service all non-Aryans (which meant any person with a single Jewish parent or grandparent). Bar associations were prohibited from admitting additional non-Aryans to membership or from granting existing non-Aryan members permission to practice law any longer. Patients insured by the national medical insurance program would not have their expenses reimbursed if they consulted non-Aryan doctors. Jewish enrollment in German high schools was restricted. A Jewish student was defined as a child with a single Jewish grandparent.

The Jews were the only group singled out for a total systematic annihilation by the Nazis. Theoretically, a Jew could escape the death sentence imposed by the Nazis only by leaving Nazi-occupied Europe, since every Jew was marked for death. By contrast, the families of other enemies of the Third Reich were usually not held liable. If one particular individual of non-Jewish background or extraction was executed or sent to a concentration camp, it did not necessarily follow that members of his family would meet the same fate. Entire

Jewish families, however, were implicated in the guilt of any of their members.

Although the German population was not unanimously in agreement with Hitler's persecution of the Jews, there is no evidence of any organized or large-scale protests regarding their treatment. There were Germans who defied the strict boycott of Jews and purposely bought in Jewish stores, and there were those who aided Jews to escape and to hide; but their number was very small.

The various steps taken by the Nazis prior to the Final Solution were all done in public and were therefore disclosed in the press. Foreign correspondents reported on all the major anti-Jewish actions legislated by the Nazis in Germany, Austria, and Czechoslovakia prior to World War II. After the war began, further information became difficult to obtain; nonetheless, reports were published regarding the fate of the Jews. Although the Nazis did not publicize the Final Solution, details of the murders began to filter through to the West less than one year after the systematic slaughter of Jews was begun.

Two out of three European Jews were murdered, women and children included. In contrast, battlefield losses for the Russians were one in 22, for the Germans, one in 25; for the British, one in 150. The Jews did not suffer as ordinary citizens of defeated countries; they were the recipients of "special treatment," ruthlessly and cruelly uprooted from their homes and families and sent away to be killed only because they were Jews.

It must be emphasized that the indifference of the non-Jewish world only accentuated the suffering of the victims at the hands of their brutal executioners. The cruelty of the enemy would have been incapable of breaking the prisoners; it was the silence of those they believed to be their friends which broke their hearts. This moral nihilism in the world at large was a sadism far more cowardly, even if more subtle. In the words of one of the most eloquent survivors of all, Elie Wiesel, "At Auschwitz not only one man died, but also the idea of man. To live in a world where there is nothing any more, where the executioner acts as god, as judge—many wanted no part of it. It was its own heart the world incinerated at Auschwitz" ["A Plea for the Dead" in *Legends of Our Time* (New York: Avon, 1970)].

The Holocaust is a reason why today many Jews care more about each other than they do about other people. Not that they fail to care about others, but others are not alone. Jews are, or at least *were* alone, and might well be again. Jews are convinced that if they do not matter most to and for each other, they will matter most to no one else. It is not a surrender to cynicism or despair. For the Jewish people it is the legacy of reality they have inherited.

The experience of the Holocaust also accounts in large measure for the incomparable attachments that bind most Jews to the State of Israel wherever in the world they may live. Jews vowed that in the aftermath of the Holocaust their lives never could or would be the same. They promised themselves that the memory of the innocent millions who suffered and perished would inspire them to a rebirth of Jewish vitality and renewal. They pledged that the death of the victims would begin a new period of redemption for all the survivors, which included Jews everywhere.

That promise became fulfillment in the rebirth of the State of Israel. Out of the ashes of grief and despair emerged the reestablishment of Jewish sovereignty for the first time in 2000 years and on soil that was sacred to Jews from the dawn of their history. It was a refuge and a homecoming for Jews all over the world. Here was a land saturated with memories and destined to resume in unprecedented fashion a fabulous adventure for the Jewish spirit. What world Jewry had lost could never be redeemed, but what it had gained could at least be defended.

Every Jew in every land became a signatory to that pledge as a way of renewing an ancient Covenant. Jewish survival was elevated to the category of mitzvah, a religious imperative. If in the aftermath of the Holocaust Jews failed to guard and protect the inalienable rights of the Jewish people, they would forfeit any claims of being responsible Jews. That generation would leave an indelible blight on the pages of Jewish history. The significance of Israel as a center of Jewish life will be examined in more detail below.

At most times, in most places, the Jewish people have functioned almost as a single organism. When one part hurt, all the other parts suffered. A danger to one was perceived as a danger to all. A challenge to one was considered a challenge to all. That phenomenon has been especially evident since the restoration of the State of Israel. It is difficult to find among any people an adequate analogy for the indissoluble bonds that bind the Jewish people to each other wherever they may live.

THE CHOSEN PEOPLE

The linkage across time and space among Jews everywhere inevitably leads to a consideration of this community of faith and history as the "chosen people." Invariably and unfortunately that term has been associated with references to special rank, status, or privilege. The truth is precisely the contrary. Membership in the chosen people is a distinction only of special obligations and responsibilities. It does not bestow any supreme rewards or honors upon its constituents. Being the chosen people is nothing more nor less than accepting the task of fulfilling the Covenant which derives from Sinai. The Covenant was binding not only upon the generation to which Moses delivered it in his own time and place, but upon all who descended by birth or by choice from that early band of wanderers.

Although they were "chosen," the Jewish people always acknowledged their own weaknesses and recognized their own tendency to be backsliders. The prophets repeatedly castigated them for their failures and warned them about the catastrophic consequences they would suffer by ignoring their contract with God. Eventually, their defiance of divine truth and judgment resulted in exile and expulsion from their own Promised Land; but even then, the later prophets proclaimed that the Covenant still endured, and that indeed, as a consequence of their bitter experience, the people of Israel were even better prepared to continue their service to God as the witness to His power and presence in the world. The prophet known to us only as the later Isaiah was confident that on behalf of God, the people of Israel "will bring forth justice to the nations. . . ," will bring it forth according to the truth, and "will not fail or be discouraged, till [they have] established justice in the earth. . . ." (Isa. 42:1, 3–4).

Very early in the prophetic movement, the conviction was firmly rooted that this unique relationship between God and Israel required higher standards of performance for the Jewish people than for any other. After cataloguing the punishments that will befall all the nations of the world for their own particular transgressions, the prophet Amos envisioned God's pronouncement to Israel in the harshest of terms by declaring, "'You only have I known of all the families of the earth; therefore I will punish you for all your iniquities'" (Amos 3:2).

In rabbinic literature the predicament of election as God's people is not a distinction particularly relished. The Midrash reports that the Jews were not certain they could or should accept the task of leadership God had assigned to them. Perhaps they anticipated the disheartening future it would bring them or the deprivation and the grievous burdens it would impose upon them. They began to blame Moses and the God Who had inspired him. Then it was that God told them: "If you accept My Torah, it will be well with you, but if you do not, I will pick up this mountain [Sinai], turn it upside down like a kettle, and bury you beneath it" (*Mekilta, Bahodesh* 3, 65a; *Shabbat* 88a).

There is nothing in the Bible to indicate that the Jewish people were chosen because of any inherent moral superiority. In fact, the biblical record is riddled with the transgressions and shortcomings of this people's performance. The choice of Israel is ultimately a mystery and not a reward for ethical excellence.

Indeed, it seems that moral elevation is not the reason but the goal of Israel's election. It may be more fitting, therefore, to devise a different term than "chosenness" to convey the peculiar quality of Israel's role in the divine drama of history. The most helpful source in this effort is the Hebrew phrase which actually deserves a better translation than simply "chosen people." The Hebrew term is *am segullah*, which means literally "a people of treasure" or more freely, "a treasured people, a distinguished or precious people."

This alternate designation helps to avoid overtones of exclusiveness, special rank, or status. Israel is precious to God for a particular purpose, which does not preclude the possibility that other peoples are also precious and unique for different considerations. In this context, the notion of *election* may be understood in more democratic terminology. Leaders who are elected to serve the public good are not necessarily better or wiser or purer than their constituencies. They are simply entrusted with a responsibility which rests upon them by virtue of their office. Some may serve the public good in capacities such as lawyers, physicians, teachers, or social workers, or in other honored, respected occupations.

In a similar way, the Jewish people are unique and precious, and this makes them a chosen people. In a sense they achieve this distinction not simply because God chose them, but because they themselves chose the role they serve through their readiness and determination to struggle for the truths of Torah. Others, however, may also earn that distinction of being precious and unique by virtue of their own contribution to human excellence. On this basis, most Jews will agree historically as well as theologically that they have indeed been a chosen people.

The primary task of this chosen people is to be a witness to the wisdom of divine truth. A majestic formulation of that task are these words of God proclaimed through the vision of Isaiah:

> "I am the Lord, I have called you in righteousness,
> I have taken you by the hand and kept you;
> I have given you as a covenant
> to the people,
> a light to the nations,
> to open the eyes that are blind,
> to bring out the prisoners from the dungeon,
> from the prison those who sit in darkness."
>
> [Isa. 42:6–7]

The purpose of Israel's mission is to act on God's behalf by demonstrating that their cause is universal and applies to all people. The moral mandate which they serve is not their exclusive property but a sacred trust which they are summoned to preserve for all who would follow it. That is clearly the appeal of the prophetic pronouncement:

> "You are My witnesses," says the Lord,
> "and My servant whom I have chosen,
> that you may know and believe Me
> and understand that I am He.
> Before Me no God was formed,
> nor shall there be any after Me."
>
> [Isa. 43:10]

In modern Jewish religious thought, the concept of "chosenness" has been subject to serious reassessment. One of the most prominent contemporary Jewish theologians, Dr. Mordecai M. Kaplan (1881–), has replaced the idea of "chosenness" with a doctrine of "vocation." Even Kaplan, however, emphasized that "Jewish religion would have Jewish civilization make for the enhancement not only of Jewish life but of mankind and thus help to render manifest the cosmic purpose of human life. . . . To live this is to live with a sense of vocation or calling, without involving ourselves in any of the invidious distinctions implied in the doctrine of election. . . ." (Mordecai M. Kaplan, *The Future of the American Jew* [New York: Macmillan Co., 1948], p. 229).

Kaplan later amplified this notion of social responsibility for the Jewish people and elevated it to a universal concern. He concluded: "The purpose of Jewish existence is to be a people in the image of God. The meaning of Jewish existence is to foster in ourselves as Jews, and to awaken in the rest of the world, a sense of moral responsibility in action" (Mordecai M. Kaplan, *The Purpose and Meaning of Jewish Experience* [Philadelphia: Jewish Publication Society of America, 1964], p. 318).

In Jewish tradition, as we have noted earlier, all people, regardless of race, religion, or ethnic origin, are equally God's children, equally precious in His sight, equally deserving of justice and mercy from any human agency or institution. Differences among individuals are a consequence of their personal performance. No person is inherently better than any other.

Judaism is virtually oblivious to race. Although traditional sources trace the origins of the Jewish people to the patriarchs of Israel, and although biblical evidence exists of early exclusionary practices by Israelites, kinship generally is never linked entirely to blood descent. Under existing provisions of Jewish practice, any person who chooses to join the Jewish people and to follow the Jewish faith enjoys equal status with every Jew who was born into the Covenant. No one is excluded any longer from membership because of racial or ethnic differences. The standards for entry into Judaism are admittedly demanding, but they are entirely a matter of theological, moral, ritual, and educational preparedness.

Although the requirements may be stringent, conversion to Judaism is not a precondition for salvation in this world or the next. One of the rabbis stated explicitly: "The righteous of all the world have a share in the world to come" (*Tosefta: Sanhedrin* 13.2). One chooses to become a Jew not for the purpose of achieving eternal rewards but for the purpose of building a better world. Any righteous person may expect whatever rewards accrue to justice and goodness in this world or the next.

In some ways it is even easier for a non-Jew to achieve lasting reward than for a Jew. Eligibility for the world to come requires a non-Jew to follow the seven commandments of the Covenant which God consummated with Noah. That Covenant embodies for Judaism the fundamental precepts which should govern all civilized society. It includes prohibitions against (1) idolatry, (2) incest and adultery, (3) bloodshed, (4) the profanation of God's name, (5) injustice and lawlessness, (6) robbery, and (7) inhumane conduct, such as cutting a limb from a living animal. In addition, Talmudic literature is filled with legends about heathens who supposedly "acquired the world to come" by single acts of extraordinary compassion or courage. By contrast, a Jew is traditionally expected to observe as many of the six hundred and thirteen commandments of the Torah as may apply to him if he seeks assurance of eternal life.

The recognition among Jews that others possess sufficient spiritual merit for divine approval is a unique distinction unparalleled in any Western religious tradition. It helps to explain the approach to conversion among many rabbinic authorities who will accept Jews by choice who are sincere and determined, but who will not actively seek them. Indeed, Halakah instructs a rabbi to discourage potential proselytes and to yield only if they persist in their request.

To a considerable degree, this ambivalent policy on proselytes was a product of history. During the period of the Roman Empire and before, Jewish missionaries were frequent visitors to the most remote corners of the known world. The most optimistic of them even hoped for a future in which Judaism would prevail everywhere. Unfortunately, many of those who converted to Judaism eventually wavered or attempted continuously to dilute Judaism with pagan ritual and practice. Others turned out to be fair-weather believers who abandoned their new faith as soon as it became subject to oppression and persecution. A number of them ultimately settled for less ritually demanding religions such as Mithraism and early Christianity. In later centuries, proselytizing efforts by Jews were punishable by death, according to Christian Church law. The seemingly rigorous stance of Halakah on the issue of conversion is a consequence of painful experience and a systematic attempt to ensure that newcomers to Judaism will be firm and reliable.

It should not be surprising that during the Middle Ages Jews periodically vented their anger and resentment upon their tormentors by classifying them as idolators and denying them the possibility of salvation because of their hatred and contempt for Jews. It could hardly be otherwise for Jews in a world which robbed them of every vestige of personal dignity and self-worth.

A more recent development of liberal Jewish attitudes toward non-Jews, especially in a democratic setting, is a recognition that every religious discipline contributes to the totality of spiritual truth. The quality of the whole human enterprise is better and brighter precisely because of the differences among peoples and civilizations. One culture stimulates another and encourages a continuous process of reassessment and renewal. Every religion challenges every other; each contributes some insight or value which the others cannot fully grasp or understand. Unfortunately, the reality of the human condition does not facilitate the application of this proposition; but that misfortune does not make it any less true.

For the Jewish people, the contribution of Judaism is endowed with a distinction of the highest order. The dictates of reason are an essential component in its formulation of faith. Its ethical idealism is imperishable but practical. Social justice is the heart of its message. Physical and spiritual reality are blended in a clear but gentle balance. Its legacy of language and literature, its ritual pageantry, dedication to freedom of conscience and reverence for life are all crown jewels of the human spirit.

At the same time, most liberal Jews will not pretend that Judaism has exhausted every measure of truth and goodness in the universe. Some have developed better insights into mysticism, others have concentrated more intently on the quest for peace, while still others have created more dramatic and inspiring rituals. Most religious faiths, therefore, do not compete with one another, but complement one another. Most possess their own share of truth and merit, and have a right to thrive and flourish. Out of its own unique contribution, every major faith ensures that the world is far better served with a multiplicity of beliefs than it could be out of a rigid uniformity of belief.

5
Israel: The Land

If I forget you, O Jerusalem, let my right hand wither!
Let my tongue cleave to the roof of my mouth,
if I do not remember you,
if I do not set Jerusalem above my highest joy.

Ps. 137:5–6

THE SPIRITUAL LONGING FOR ZION

Israel is not only a term that identifies the Jewish people. It is also the name of the land which has been sacred to that people since the beginning of recorded history, and it is irrevocably linked to the historic movement known as Zionism.

Zionism is more than a political phenomenon. It is an expression of Jewish religious belief and hope, because it reflects the most cherished components of Jewish faith. It is a profoundly spiritual expression of fidelity to the Covenant which links God and Israel, both people and land. That union is the most distinctive quality of Jewish spirituality. In many ways, therefore, Zionism and Judaism, as the religion of the Jewish people, are synonymous. Those who condemn Zionism also condemn Judaism. Anti-Zionism is not far removed from anti-Semitism.

On November 11, 1975, the United Nations General Assembly passed a resolution equating Zionism with racism. That shameful distortion of mankind's oldest quest for freedom and independence was roundly condemned by those with even a minimal understanding of its origins and purpose. Zionism is the embodiment of the highest and noblest aspirations of the Jewish people from the beginning of its history.

Dr. Yosef Tekoah, Israel's ambassador to the United Nations at the time, responded to the outrage by stating:

> Zionism is the love of Zion. Zionism is the Jewish people's liberation movement, the quest for freedom, for equality with other nations. Yet, in an organization in which liberation movements are hailed and supported, the Jewish people's struggle to restore its independence and sovereignty is maligned and slandered in an endless spate of malice and venom.

An understanding of Jewish history and the Jewish people's abiding passion for the Land of Israel requires an appreciation for biblical events in the context of the Covenant which bound the people to their sacred soil. Moses, Joshua, the Judges, kings, and prophets all labored in the abiding conviction that the destiny of their people was irretrievably tied to the Land of Israel. This parcel of earth became not only the home of the Jewish soul, but the focus of its aspirations. Once the roots had been planted, they could never again be plucked out.

The religious significance of Israel to Jews cannot be restricted only to the period of the patriarchs and prophets. When the Babylonians conquered Judah in 586 B.C.E. and expelled Jewish leaders to Babylon, there followed a period of subjugation known in Jewish history as "the Exile." The people had become so attached to the Land of Israel that, in the midst of their grief, the exiles composed their most eloquent lament. The words of Psalm 137 underscore their longing to return. They did not forget Jerusalem.

Quite unexpectedly, the misfortune of the Exile had a beneficial effect on the Jewish people. They emerged from it more unified than ever before. After their return to the land and during the long period of Persian and Greek domination, they still exercised the right of local autonomy consistent with the policy of the prevailing power. During this time, from 522 B.C.E. to 168 B.C.E., they composed some of their greatest religious literature, including the Book of Daniel, the larger portion of the Psalmistic literature, and the beginnings of the apocalyptic writings in such books as Joel, Zechariah, and the latter portions of Isaiah and Ezekiel.

By the beginning of the second century B.C.E., the Jewish people in Palestine (then called Judea) were caught as pawns between the rival Seleucid and Ptolemaic empires. Still, they refused to compromise their religious or national sovereignty and struggled to preserve their independent status. History recorded that struggle as the Maccabean Revolt (168–165 B.C.E.), which developed into the story of Hanukkah. The success of that effort led to the founding of the Hasmonean dynasty, which endured for 140 years. The strength of the dynasty rested on the conviction that the Jewish people in their own land could again achieve complete self-government and self-determination.

Rome eventually succeeded Greece as the supreme political power in the Near East, and its oppressive rule of Judea culminated in the destruction of Jerusalem and the Temple in 70 C.E. Even though Jewish self-rule had ended earlier with the invasion of Pompey in 63 C.E., the Jews stubbornly refused to capitulate or to abandon their own homeland. Determined resistance continued until the defeat of Simon Bar Kochba in 135 C.E. after a major military campaign against Roman tyranny. More important, in spite of the fact that the vast majority of Jews were dispersed throughout the known world, a persistent remnant, sometimes numbering in the tens of thousands, remained on their native soil for the next eighteen hundred years.

After the destruction of the Second Jewish Commonwealth by the Romans in 70 C.E., the daily prayer book became the voice of Zionism. Despite the wide scattering of the Jews, the hope and conviction that Zion would be restored was never abandoned. In this manner every Jew in the world expressed the plea for the rebuilding of Jerusalem. Three times daily, every day in the year for nearly nineteen centuries, Jews prayed: "May our eyes behold Thy return to Zion in mercy. . . . Praised are Thou, O Lord, Who wilt bring back His presence to Zion."

For just as many centuries Jews have also prayed: "May a redeemer come to Zion." Every year at the Passover seder and at the end of the Day of Atonement every Jew would cry out, "Next year in Jerusalem!" Everywhere in the Jewish prayer book, whether on the Sabbath, a festival, or any ordinary weekday, there is hardly a point in the service that lacks a fervent expression of the hope that the Jewish people dispersed to the four corners of the earth will be gathered and brought back to Zion, the land of their beginnings.

At marriage ceremonies everywhere over the course of countless centuries, the hope was expressed not only that the couple under the wedding canopy would be happy, but that, in the words of the prophet, "Soon there might be heard in the countryside of Judea and the streets of Jerusalem the glad sound of rejoicing of bridegroom and bride."

At every Jewish funeral, God was invoked to comfort the bereaved in the present circumstances along with "all those who mourn for Zion."

Jews in exile, as strangers in every country of the world until relatively recent times, found enormous religious meaning in the hope of the return to Zion. Desperately they longed for the moment to justify their age-old conviction that God had not forsaken them as non-Jews said He had, and to demonstrate that their two thousand years of history on the land, the Covenant, and both commonwealths were neither accidental nor in vain. They longed for the moment of return to confirm their belief that the Covenant still remained valid and would be fulfilled.

MODERN ZIONISM

Throughout the period of dispersion, charismatic leaders and would-be messiahs continually emerged to give political emphasis to Jewish spiritual yearnings for return. It was not, however, until the pogroms and massacres of Eastern European Jews by the Russian Czars in the late 1880s and early 1900s that these sporadic aspirations began to coalesce into a political force.

The man who, more than any other, wove together a tapestry of modern Jewish nationalism out of the strands of persecution, religious history, and political reality was Theodor Herzl. In 1894, Herzl was sent to Paris to cover the trial of Alfred Dreyfus, a Jewish army officer, for the Vienna *Neue Freie Presse.*

Alfred Dreyfus attained the rank of captain in the French officer corps and was attached to the general staff of the French army. In 1894, he was accused of selling highly classified military secrets to Germany. The evidence leading to the indictment was later unmasked as a deliberate fraud based completely on forged documents.

The Dreyfus affair was a classic paradigm of the relentless power struggle between the Church and supporters of the French monarchy on one side and the forces for reform on the other. Despite his complete innocence, Dreyfus was tried by a military court, convicted, and sentenced to life imprisonment on Devil's Island in French Guiana.

This miscarriage of justice was contested by a minority group consisting mostly of intellectuals who called themselves the Dreyfusards. The case was reopened after Colonel Georges Picquart discovered that the trial documents were all forgeries. He demanded a new hearing for Dreyfus by a civil tribunal, not a military court. Supporters for the petition included the most illustrious names in all France, such as the novelist Anatole France, the statesman Georges Clemenceau, the scholar Joseph Reinach, and the socialist Jean Jaures.

The most strenuous statement of outrage issued from the pen of the prominent French novelist Emile Zola, who courageously risked his fame and reputation when he published an open letter to the President of the French Republic and chose for the title of the message his opening words, *''J'Accuse''* (*''I Accuse''*). Zola openly denounced the general staff of the army for being in league with forgers and conspirators and dismissed the verdict of the court martial as ''a crime of high treason against humanity.''

Eventually a tidal wave of public opinion compelled the military to reconsider its decision in the Dreyfus case and after brief deliberation, reduce his sentence to ten years imprisonment. Emile Zola had been jailed but had escaped to London. Public repudiations of the verdict persisted, and efforts continued unabated to vindicate Dreyfus. Finally, in 1906 the civil supreme court of France completely exonerated Alfred Dreyfus and restored him to his former rank in the French officer corps.

The experience of this case stunned Theodor Herzl with an awareness of how grievously anti-Semitism had infected France and central Europe. He concluded that there could be no future for Jews so long as they remained in the midst and at the mercy of a larger, hostile, non-Jewish world. He returned to Vienna convinced that no amount of assimilation could alleviate this condition. The Jews, in his view, were not merely a religious entity, but a people. Therefore they required and deserved a state of their own. Herzl formulated his classic vision of political Zionism in a short book, *Der Jüdische Staat (The Jewish State)*, which was published in 1896. Several years later, in 1902, he composed a novel which he entitled *Alt-Neu Land (The Old-New Land)*; it was a fanciful, romantic tale, written primarily to help pay off some of the indebtedness the new movement had incurred.

In 1897 Herzl convened the first Zionist Congress in Basel, Switzerland. The occasion marked the first time in more than eighteen hundred years, since the collapse of the Great Sanhedrin, that a Jewish body was convened to deliberate and direct the future of the Jewish people.

The results of that Congress produced the Basel Program which stipulated that "the object of Zionism is to establish for the Jewish people a publicly and legally assured home in Palestine." Herzl soon afterward wrote in his diary that "at Basel, I founded the Jewish state. . . ."

THE RESTORATION OF JEWISH SOVEREIGNTY

While Zionist spokesmen labored to secure world endorsement for the restoration of a Jewish state, Herzl's initiative triggered a resurgence of Jewish settlement in Palestine, especially among East European Jews. The term *aliyah* ("going up") became the modern Hebrew word for immigration. The settlers of the future Jewish homeland were classified by the particular period of aliyah in which they had arrived, beginning with the First Aliyah (1880–1905) and continuing through the Second (1905–1914), the Third (1919–1924), the Fourth (1924–1929), and the Fifth (1933–1939). Many of the early immigrants especially transformed the barren wilderness of their ancient Holy Land into a thriving, fruitful oasis, primarily by creating and developing a new ideal in Jewish life, the *kibbutz,* a collective agricultural settlement based upon joint ownership of the means of production and equality in the distribution of benefits.

The young Jewish community in Palestine called itself the *Yishuv* ("the settlement"). By the eve of World War I, the evidence of Jewish rebirth in this corner of the Middle East was impossible to ignore. What was for centuries a desolate wasteland was now flourishing beyond the most hopeful predictions. In 1880 only 25,000 Jews inhabited the land and survived mostly on charity in four "holy" cities. By 1914 the population had doubled, and the vast majority were supporting themselves. The Zionist movement gained rapid momentum and attracted a steadily growing constituency.

In 1917, largely through the efforts of Dr. Chaim Weizmann, Great Britain issued the famous Balfour Declaration promising "the establishment in Palestine of a national homeland for the Jewish people." At the conclusion of hostilities the League of Nations, in accord with the Treaty of Versailles, entrusted to Britain in 1920 a mandate to govern Palestine according to the terms of the Balfour Declaration. Two years later, this arrangement was endorsed by thirty-three nations of the world.

Unfortunately, the linguistic ambiguities of the British document, which did not promise that Palestine would be *the* national home *of* the Jewish people, enabled Jews and Arabs to interpret the statement in opposite ways. The British stalled continuously in their pledge to establish Jewish sovereignty and eventually, in the face of intense Arab opposition, terminated all Jewish immigration to Palestine. In 1939 they called the mandate unworkable and claimed they had already fulfilled the terms of the Balfour Declaration.

The Yishuv nonetheless stood firm. Between two World Wars (1918–1939), the Jewish community in Palestine increased eight times in size. One-third of the entire population now included Jews. Over 225,000 Jews found refuge in Palestine from Nazi tyranny. Thousands more arrived there from Hungary, Poland, Austria, Rumania, and other lands of persecution. Jewish farmers produced three times as much as in the period before the British mandate. Palestine became the world's second largest exporter of oranges. Modern Jewish cities such as Tel Aviv and Eilat mushroomed out of a barren wilderness. Jewish immigrants harnessed electric power from the Jordan River, extracted rich mineral deposits from the Dead Sea, built railroads, highways, and even a new harbor for the city of Haifa.

Most important of all was the united community into which the Jews of Palestine molded themselves. In spite of enormous differences in lands of origin, in their customs, dress, and beliefs, they still managed to achieve an amazing level of solidarity. They governed themselves in religion and education. They collected their own taxes, developed defense forces, organized political campaigns and elections, and established enviable standards of health care and medical services.

In the span of only fifty years, a leader came, a movement began, and pioneers reclaimed the neglected soil of their ancestors. The world displayed some kindness and understanding but for the most part supported the venture grudgingly or not at all. On the eve of World War II, Jews had regained some of their ancient homeland, but were still a minority and powerless to shape their own future.

Not until 1947 would the United Nations finally acknowledge the right of the Jewish people to self-determination by proclaiming a partition of Palestine into both Jewish and Arab states. That historic decision was the turning point that enabled a spiritual dream to become a spectacular reality.

Herzl did not live long enough to see his dream materialize. He died in 1904. By any standard of tangible achievement, Herzl accomplished little. He won no dazzling diplomatic victories. Support for his political activism remained lukewarm, even in the Jewish community. Nonetheless, he was a genuine visionary for the renewal of the Jewish people and a gifted architect for the political structure to achieve Zionist goals. He reawakened the prospects for Jewish sovereignty and turned sentimental and philanthropic hopes into practical channels.

Political Zionism is the irreplaceable vehicle for the practical fulfillment of all the centuries of prayer in which longings and yearnings were voiced for the reestablishment of the Jewish people as a nation in the Land of Israel. All messianic concepts in Judaism are tied to this hope. In Jewish tradition, the Messiah was he who would lead the people of Israel back to the land of their origins where once again they would be reconstituted as a nation. The irrefutable proof of his credentials as the Messiah would be precisely this task of reviving the Jewish people as a national political entity in their ancient homeland.

Israel is born of an idea—the idea of an historic reunion of God, His people, and their land for the purpose of fulfilling the terms of their Covenant. Judaism is not the only religion with a homeland. Every great historic faith has a geographic center. There were many such religious centers, vast areas of the globe where whole nations progressed and nurtured their faith and religious culture.

Roman Catholics turn to Rome and the Vatican. The Episcopal

Church finds its home in England, Presbyterianism in Scotland, Lutheranism in Germany and Switzerland, Islam in most of North Africa and West Asia. While some of these religions may only be tolerated in some lands, they are the official dominant faith in several places. Judaism remains so in only one: the State of Israel.

The ties of the Jewish people to Israel are in some respects even more binding than those of other peoples to their lands of origin. In most cases the major claim to inheritance is political. For Jews the issue is more than politics. It is a matter of religious, ethnic and historic roots in soil which centuries of precious love have sanctified. To the Jewish people the Land of Israel is a unique, theological phenomenon, part of the eternal Covenant and of more than political importance. It is a moral imperative, as the prophet envisioned, "For out of Zion shall go forth the Law, and the word of the Lord from Jerusalem" (Isa. 2:3).

The imperishable attachments of the Jewish people to the Land of Israel do not preclude an equivalent emphasis upon the vitality of Jewish life in the Diaspora, in free democratic countries where Judaism flourishes in an open and creative society. The increasing volume and quality of Jewish culture in North America, including programs of higher Jewish education, religious studies, day schools, community organization, and activism in behalf of deeper, stronger bonds among Jews everywhere attest to the dynamic agenda of the Jewish community outside as well as inside the State of Israel. The Jewish homeland is a continuing inspiration to all of world Jewry, but the vision and promise of a Jewish future in every friendly climate and country remain a major focus for most Jews.

The attachment of the Jewish people to Israel is but a reflection of their larger, unbounded commitment to Judaism as it functions through the Covenant. Land and people are intricately interwoven into the fabric of Jewish belief and practice. Observance of the Torah and its divine mandate presuppose an enduring affinity of the people for their Promised Land in perpetuity. That is what makes their compact with God an eternal Covenant.

PART TWO

THE INTERPRETATIONS

1
Reform Judaism

Reform Judaism does more than tolerate diversity; it engenders it. In our uncertain historical situation we must expect to have far greater diversity than previous generations knew. How we shall live with diversity without stifling dissent and without paralyzing our ability to take positive action will test our character and our principles. We stand open to any position thoughtfully and conscientiously advocated in the spirit of Reform Jewish beliefs.

[*A Centenary Perspective of Reform Judaism* edited by Eugene Borowitz (New York: Union of American Hebrew Congregations, 1974).]

Reform Judaism began in Europe about 1810. The first motivation of this movement was the desire of the emancipated Jew to find a place in two worlds, the Jewish community and the land of residence. The early Reformer wanted to be both a Jew and a German, a Jew and a Frenchman, a Jew and an Englishman, or a Jew and an American. In the beginning, the Reformers succeeded at least in some measure. The undertaking was novel and intriguing, both to them and to their Christian neighbors.

The second major goal of the Reform movement was an attempt to adapt Jewish law (Halakah) to new requirements. The emphasis at the outset was on adaptability, not on total rejection. The early Reformers understood very well that Jewish law was central to Jewish life. They acknowledged the need to discontinue the observance of antiquated commandments, but they staunchly defended the necessity of the legal process in determining Jewish belief and practice. Unlike their Orthodox opposition, however, they insisted that since Jewish law had been developed by rabbinic teachers, it was a human mandate, not a divine one. As such, it was not immutable. It was subject to change as time and place required.

The early Reformers selected as their first goal the introduction of limited changes in worship and ritual. Every one of their proposals, strangely enough, was subject to the closest scrutiny of Jewish law. Every modification was defended and explained in an avalanche of scholarly responses. One of the first innovations was the presentation of the sermon in the vernacular. That single, modest proposal launched the famous Leopold Zunz, an architect of Reform thought, on a monumental achievement in scholarship dealing with the development of sermonics and preaching in Judaism.

The early Reformers also chose to introduce the organ into the synagogue service. They subsequently investigated the question of musical accompaniment in Jewish law and traced the subject all the way back to ancient Temple days when it was part of every service. And so it continued.

The original Reform movement, known as ''classical'' Reform, lasted for about two generations. It flourished mostly in Germany, less so in France and England, and much less in Hungary and Italy. When it reached the New World, it underwent a radical transformation.

There were ample reasons for such a complete and total transition. America was fertile ground for intellectual and spiritual freedom of every dimension. In the mid-nineteenth century especially, the individualism of the frontier was strong and dominated every phase of ordinary life. It was literally every man for himself, according to his mind and his might. Every fine distinction prompted a quest for total independence.

In Judaism, the challenge was not only individualism but rationalism, the irresistible power of reason which subjected every conventional religious claim to a test of universal truth. In addition, American individualism was closely allied to a general mood of optimism and universalism, both of which were two-edged swords. Though they promised a coming age of unheralded peace and prosperity, they also brought in their wake a world of hidden potential dangers. Individualism was prone to lawlessness; optimism could lead to complacency; and universalism was often an excuse for escape from one's self and the evasion of commitment to the Jewish people. Eventually, in America, those dangers came to pose a formidable threat to the continuity of Reform Judaism within the mainstream of Jewish life.

The classical Reform that began in Germany ended in 1881 with the formulation of the Pittsburgh Platform. This was a statement of principles for Reform Judaism conceived by a group of Reform rabbis without any official endorsement by the Reform movement. It came to be the definitive posture of Reform Judaism for more than half a century. The most sensational features of the Pittsburgh Platform were its rejection of Hebrew, the dietary laws, and many other traditional rituals, and its repudiation of Zionist sentiments.

The Pittsburgh Platform, however, also highlighted the failure of the two major efforts of classical Reform which had characterized the movement in Europe. That failure transformed the American version from "classical" Reform to "radical" Reform. Classical Reform tried to find a place in two worlds for the Jew. Radical Reform, formalized in the Pittsburgh Platform, declared there could be only one world; that was the world of one's citizenship, the country to which one pledged allegiance. In America it was the American ethic which totally subordinated the claims of Jewish tradition. Judaism might merit nominal loyalty by radical Reformers, but they did not really believe that a Jew could live in any meaningful way in two worlds at the same time.

The other principle of earlier Reform had been a commitment to evolution in Jewish law, not revolution. Classical Reform tried to adapt Jewish law to new conditions while still retaining the principle. The Pittsburgh Platform abandoned that effort altogether. Halakah, the Hebrew word for "Jewish law," disappeared from Reform vocabulary. Even the word *mitzvah* vanished from Reform conversation, except for an occasional reference to bar mitzvah. Radical Reform demanded only that Jews accept the authority of ethical injunctions and that they live in conformity with the teachings of the Prophets. Not even these principles were reinforced by any association with established norms or necessity for action. In fact, they were all much more a matter of theoretical commitment than living realities.

Rationalization, individualism, optimism, universalism, and class distinction were the background against which radical Reform

Judaism entrenched itself in the upper strata of the American Jewish community in the nineteenth century. Halakah was gone, mitzvah was gone, and the Jew now lived, or attempted to live, in the gentile community. To accomplish that goal, he necessarily diminished his concern for the Jewish people. With the loss of peoplehood, Jewish law, and personal discipline, little was left. Radical Reformers scheduled a weekly service which was held usually on the Sabbath (Saturday) but in some instances on Sunday, and Reform Jews were especially pleased if gentiles would attend to hear their rabbi's sermon. They operated a Sunday school and introduced confirmation; those were the limits of their expectations for most of the nineteenth century and the earlier part of our twentieth century.

Radical Reform, with its rejection of Hebrew, headcoverings, and Zionism, coupled with its emphasis on decorum and Sunday morning services, lasted until the late 1920s and the early 1930s. The gathering stormclouds over Nazi Europe began to convince them as nothing else could that the centrality of peoplehood was still a cardinal precept for Jewish survival. Differences in affiliation failed to save Jews anywhere in Europe. With or without *yamulkes* ("headcoverings"), all met the same fate.

In addition, the appeal of Reform Judaism to children of East European immigrants, saturated with traditional beliefs and practices, gradually modified the extreme liberation of the movement. The new generation of Reform Jews was eager to restore a balance between Jewish particularism and universalism.

All the hopes and dreams about the imminent arrival of the Messianic Age which emerged with enthusiasm in the nineteenth century began to disintegrate in the bread lines and soup kitchens of the Depression, later in the ashes of Auschwitz and Buchenwald of the Nazi Era and World War II. It was time to retrace a few steps and reassess the criteria for future decisions about beliefs and practices.

A major consequence of that reappraisal was the Columbus Platform of 1937 which replaced the Pittsburgh Platform of 1881 as the dominant statement of Reform Judaism. It was formulated and endorsed in Columbus, Ohio, at the annual convention of the Central Conference of American Rabbis. The Union of American Hebrew Congregations later ratified all of the Columbus Platform except its support for the return to Palestine.

The most controversial provisions of the Columbus Platform were its affirmation of Zionism and proposals to restore Hebrew to the worship service, traditional customs and ceremonies to homes and synagogue, and to renew the commitment to the teachings of the past and their application to the present.

The Columbus Platform, however, was not the culmination of this major reappraisal in Reform Judaism. It was only the beginning. It would take more than ten years, to the actual establishment of the State of Israel, before Reform Judaism as a movement would reflect the transformation which these new directions implied. The revolution was over, but the process of consolidation had only begun. Some Reform congregations resisted the changes for years to come, but the agony of the Holocaust and the glory of Israel reborn clearly established the necessity for serious reassessment.

To register adamant opposition to the increasing support for Zionism in the Reform movement, a small segment of rabbinic and lay leadership organized the American Council for Judaism (ACJ) in 1943. Its original purpose was to define Judaism exclusively in religious terms and repudiate any associations with nationalism. Although most rabbis and lay people resigned from the Council when it soon shifted from a posture of responsible opposition to desperate diatribe, it remained for many years a great source of embarrassment and irritation to many Jews. The ACJ has now shrunk to little more than a paper organization and exercises little if any influence at all in Jewish life or in U.S. government circles. It was once very powerful in the State Department and Defense Department especially in the mid- to late 1940s, and even later on into the 1950s.

Reform congregations even today continue the process of reforming in every realm of religious observance. They do not hesitate to change not only the practices of Orthodoxy but also the earlier practices of Reform itself. Evident in Reform Judaism is a growing tendency to create new ceremonies as well as to rejuvenate old ones. In addition to confirmation, most Reform congregations now observe a ceremony of consecration to celebrate the initial entry of children into religious school and the beginning of their Jewish education. This observance is actually rooted in a more traditional practice of acclaiming the first day of a child's religious instruction. Interest in Hebrew language now far surpasses any learning levels of previous years. Because Reform Judaism is a process and not an end product, it is most appropriate to designate it as "Reform" Judaism rather than "Reformed" Judaism.

In spite of its changing character from one generation to another, certain essential principles of Reform Judaism remain firm in any given period of time. The first is the freedom of any generation to examine existing practice and to change it for sound and sufficient reasons. It is not so much a question of how much or how well a person observed Jewish customs and ceremonies, but why. One person may observe the whole range of dietary laws and Sabbath rituals and still be Reform, while another may ignore them all and still be Orthodox. The one who believes that ceremonies are a useful means to the end of deepening attachments to Judaism but can be changed if their utility no longer functions, is a Reform Jew even if he follows traditional patterns of practice. On the other hand, the individual who contends that all ceremonial laws are divine injunctions, immutable and infallible, is theologically an Orthodox Jew even if that person observes none of them. Reform Judaism defends this distinction on the premise that the prophets themselves assigned a higher priority to the moral law than they did to the ritual law. Reform Judaism cites statements such as: ". . . I did not speak to your fathers or command them concerning burnt offerings and sacrifices. But this command I gave them, 'Obey My voice and I will be your God and you shall be My people; and walk in all the way that I command you. . . .'" (Jer. 7:22–23).

A second prevailing principle of Reform is the right to modify public worship for the purpose of enriching the experience of communal prayer. Depending upon time and place, that purpose may merit more Hebrew or less Hebrew. It may call for a standard, conventional structure or more innovative, creative worship. In little more than a hundred years of existence in America, the most widely used prayer book in Reform congregations has changed at least four times; and the instruments of worship will probably continue to evolve in every succeeding generation.

Finally, a dominant principle of Reform has been its emphasis upon the mission of social justice inherent in our biblical legacy. The Reform movement has insisted upon the application of the ethical mandate of the Hebrew prophets to the political, economic, and international problems of our time. Of all major Jewish religious movements in America, Reform Judaism is the only one with an organized voice of social conscience in Washington by way of the Religious Action Center. The supreme significance of this principle in Reform teaching derives from a multitude of prophetic precedents such as the summons of Isaiah: "'I am the Lord, I have called you in righteousness, I have taken you by the hand and kept you; I have given you as a covenant to the people, a light to the nations, to open the eyes that are blind, to bring out the prisoners from the dungeon, from the prison those who sit in darkness,'" (Isa. 42:6–7).

This stress on right conduct as the path to human fulfillment is perhaps the precept in Judaism most central to Reform. Contrary to the mood of pessimism which prevailed elsewhere, Reform Judaism looked upon world Jewry not as a community of homeless wanderers, but as an irresistible force in the world, a powerful ally in the service of liberalism and human brotherhood. That faith has endured severe testing in recent decades, but it remains a cornerstone of the structure of Reform belief and its understanding of the Covenant. Reform Judaism is predicated upon the conviction that Judaism has a permanent and noble task to perform in the world. That task is to achieve the triumph of justice, peace, and freedom for all peoples.

Among the many astounding achievements of Rabbi Isaac Mayer Wise, founder of Reform Judaism in America, was his work as its organizational catalyst. Wise concluded very early in his career that the survival of American Judaism would hinge largely on a united effort. Jewish religious life in his day hovered on the brink of chaos due to a lack of institutional cohesion. After pondering the desperate need for an organized Jewish community, Wise activated his plan for the establishment of the first intercongregational body in American Judaism. He called it the Union of American Hebrew Congregations (UAHC). The Union was formally launched in 1873 with a membership of thirty-four congregations from the South and West which had been most receptive to Wise's influence. Before long many of the leading synagogues of the East, including moderate congregations, also joined Wise's venture. From the beginning, the Union was not founded on any hierarchical system but served a facilitating function as a coordinating body in which all constituent congregations retained their complete independence. The UAHC eventually absorbed the Board of Delegates of American Israelites, which was formed in 1859 to defend the rights of Jews throughout the world. Although Wise originally intended to unite all American synagogues under the aegis of the Union, the invitation to affiliation appealed almost exclusively to liberal congregations.

The first goal which Wise envisaged for the UAHC was the creation of a theological seminary, an accredited institution of higher Jewish learning in America. Wise had campaigned for many years to establish a school for the training of rabbis brought up in the American culture. After an earlier failure in such an effort, Wise achieved success with the official opening of the Hebrew Union College on October 3, 1875, at the Plum Street Temple in Cincinnati. Wise himself spent the larger portion of his own career in Cincinnati, Ohio, which understandably became the center of American Reform Judaism. He served the College as its first President until his death in 1900. The school opened its doors with thirteen students and three faculty members. The curriculum encompassed four years of pre-Rabbinic training and an equal period of advanced study culminating in ordination. The first class completed its program in 1883. Like the UAHC, the College was designed originally to serve the needs of all Jewish congregations in America; but it soon became a seminary for Reform rabbis only. At the same time, however, it also became an influence for the founding of rabbinical seminaries by the other major movements of American Judaism.

In 1950, the Hebrew Union College merged with the Jewish Institute of Religion in New York, which had been founded by Rabbi Stephen S. Wise in 1922. HUC-JIR is now the oldest institution of Jewish higher education in the Western hemisphere and has campuses in Los Angeles and Jerusalem as well as in Cincinnati and New York. The Jerusalem branch originated as the Nelson Glueck Postgraduate School of Biblical Archaeology. It has since developed into the central facility of a first-year program for almost all entering rabbinical students, focusing primarily on the learning of Hebrew and the fostering of Biblical studies.

Wise's hope of effecting the organization of a national rabbinic body failed to materialize until several classes had completed their rabbinic training at the Hebrew Union College. Even though he had longed to establish an association for all American rabbis, he at least successfully unified his own graduates into a professional group, the Central Conference of American Rabbis (CCAR). The Conference first met in Detroit in 1889 together with the convention of the Union of American Hebrew Congregations. Wise was also elected to serve as the first president of the CCAR, a post he continued to hold to the end of his days.

Today the CCAR includes both men and women in its membership and serves in many ways on their behalf. It is the principal voice for the collective decisions of the entire body. It is a major publisher of liturgical, homiletic, and scholarly books as well as a quarterly journal for rabbis and lay people. It sponsors an extensive system of service committees, commissions, and representative delegations to other Jewish organizations.

HUC-JIR not only trains men and women as rabbis, having ordained its first female candidate in 1972, but is also a school for cantors, archeologists, educators and communal workers. Its curriculum includes advanced study for doctoral degrees in a wide range of Jewish studies.

The libraries of HUC-JIR are among the largest in the Jewish world. Together their holdings exceed 500,000 volumes and more than 6000 ancient manuscripts. The American Jewish Archives on the Cincinnati campus houses more than four million pages of documented materials. Its Periodical Center is a major repository for research in American Jewry.

At the present time, the UAHC encompasses a membership of more than 725 Reform congregations. In 1952 it transferred its administrative headquarters from Cincinnati to New York, the center of the largest concentration of Jews in the United States. The national offices of the UAHC, as well as its organizational and publishing apparatus, are located in a single Manhattan building, which also houses the National Federation of Temple Sisterhoods and similar federations of brotherhoods and youth, the commissions of education, worship, and social action, and the offices of the World Union for Progressive Judaism.

In 1976 the CCAR adopted the first restatement of Reform Jewish thought since the Columbus Platform of 1937 which it titled "A Centenary Perspective." Among its provisions, the statement acknowleged the shattering impact of the Holocaust of 1933–45 on the past generation and its irreversible significance for all future ages. As devastating as that nightmare had been, so however, was the rebirth of Jewish sovereignty in Israel in 1948 as an unsurpassed source of joy and fulfillment. Support for Zionist goals now advanced to the level of encouragement for *aliyah* (''immigration'' to Israel) and the establishment of *ARZA*, the Hebrew term meaning ''to the land'' and an acronym for American Reform Zionist Association. One of ARZA's initial projects was the promotion of *Yahel* (''flashing light''), the first Reform kibbutz in Israel, as well as a campaign to achieve equal recognition for non-Orthodox expressions of Judaism in the Jewish state.

In 1975 the CCAR published a new prayer book, *Shaarei Tefillah* (''Gates of Prayer''), which marked the first revision of the *Union Prayer Book* since 1940. One edition of the new prayer book is even available in a Hebrew format opening from right to left. The prayer book includes a memorial service for the Holocaust and a special commemoration for Israel Independence Day. Unusual additions are the benedictions for putting on the *tallith* and *tefillin*, the traditional prayer shawl and phylacteries which were rarely worn in earlier periods of Reform Judaism. The CCAR has also published its own guide for Sabbath observance in Reform Judaism, a revised manual for celebrating holidays and personal milestones at home, and a volume for the festival cycle.

Reform Judaism strives to maintain a balance between change and continuity. Some directions it pursues are familiar, others less so, but in every instance it offers a vision of the Covenant that is constantly evolving and is never static. It is likely to retain that vision at the heart of its message.

2
Conservative Judaism

The maintenance of the twin principles of authority and development in Jewish law . . . together with the emphasis upon the worldwide peoplehood of Israel—these are the basic postulates of Conservative Judaism.

Robert Gordis (1908–)

The origins of Conservative Judaism in America are generally attributed to the pioneering labors of an innovative organizer in the early nineteenth century by the name of Isaac Leeser. Leeser was a German immigrant who first settled in Richmond, Virginia, in 1824 and who began almost immediately a career as the assistant *chazzan* (''minister'') of the Sephardic congregation in Richmond. He moved to Philadelphia in 1830 to become the chazzan of the prominent Sephardic synagogue, *Mikveh Israel*.

Leeser began his innovative operations at Mikveh Israel with the introduction of English prayers and an English sermon into the standard Hebrew service. This earned him the distinction of being the first Jewish preacher in America. Leeser achieved even wider prominence, however, with his publication in 1843 of *The Occident and Jewish Advocate*, which is regarded by most historians as the first national Jewish journal in America. Leeser edited the periodical himself, and though it was largely an articulate defense of Orthodoxy in a new American setting, the issues of *The Occident* probably remain the most fruitful and insightful account available of this critical period in American Jewish history.

Leeser was also the guiding inspiration for the founding of the first American Jewish Publication Society, which collapsed six years later after a fatal fire. He designed educational curricula and materials for the earliest religious schools and translated both the Sephardic and Ashkenazic prayer books into English for better comprehension.

His crowning achievement, however, was his English translation of the Hebrew Bible in 1853. This remained the definitive Jewish version until 1917, when the Jewish Publication Society issued its own edition. In some congregations Leeser's text still prevails to this day.

Isaac Leeser directed the development of the first rabbinical school in America, Maimonides College in Philadelphia. Although it failed after six years, it still predated the efforts of Isaac Mayer Wise in Cincinnati and in its short period of existence produced the first rabbis to be trained in the United States.

Both in ideology and practice, Leeser was clearly an Orthodox Jew. Nonetheless, while he rejected what he considered to be the excesses of Reform, he still maintained that Orthodoxy was not totally bereft of potential for growth and accommodation. His confidence in this capacity for adaptation inspired him in his search for a platform that would unite all American Jews regardless of their distinctions.

Toward this end, he welcomed the efforts of Isaac Mayer Wise in organizing a single collective body that would incorporate all Jewish congregations in America. Leeser was eager to achieve a consensus in Judaism that would permit dissent without risking a rupture into various factions. That was in large measure his meaning and purpose in coining the term "catholic Israel," the totality of the Jewish people in all their diversity, a notion that the famous scholar and Jewish educator, Solomon Schechter, would amplify and emphasize. Leeser's determination, however, to seek the broadest base for perpetuating the vitality of Jewish tradition in America was clearly the initial impulse for the evolution of Conservative Judaism.

When Leeser retired from the pulpit of Mikveh Israel in 1850, he was followed by a Sephardic Jew of Italian origin, Sabbato Morais. Morais had been a student of the very prominent European scholar, Samuel David Luzzatto, had studied English in London and taught Jewish studies there at the Orphan's School of the Spanish-Portuguese Synagogue. Morais was a fiery, energetic personality whose style and manner were difficult to resist. He was, for example, an ardent abolitionist and repeatedly stated his opposition to slavery in public regardless of the repercussions in his own community. He even omitted the customary prayer in the service for the welfare of the government when he believed that national policy ignored the interests of the Jewish people.

Morais continued and expanded the pioneering efforts of Isaac Leeser in seeking a basis for lasting unity among American Jews. He aided and supported Isaac Mayer Wise in creating the Hebrew Union College, which he hoped, as Wise did, would become a center of higher Jewish learning for all segments of American Jewry. Morais even served in the administration of the college until 1885 when the terms of the Pittsburgh Platform convinced him that the polarity between the liberal and traditional sectors was impossible to resolve. In a final attempt at joint cooperation, he proposed a project among several recognized scholars for the compilation of a standard prayer book that would include traditional, Talmudic passages embellished with more recent creative materials. His proposal withered for lack of adequate encouragement or response.

Morais was spirited and resourceful enough to win the support of several colleagues in organizing still another rabbinical college in 1886, the Jewish Theological Seminary. Most of his colleagues were, like Morais, advocates of moderation in Jewish belief and practice and repudiated the extremism of early Reform. Most of them, however, by their own personal inclination, leaned toward a liberal theological stance, although they clearly parted company with the Reform movement on such issues as dietary laws, Sabbath observance, Jewish nationalism, and the importance of Hebrew.

Classes at the new seminary opened in 1887 at Shearith Israel Synagogue in New York with an enrollment of eight students. Morais was its founding president and held the office until his death. Throughout his tenure, Morais shaped the Seminary in the image of his own Sephardic Orthodoxy. The early years were exceedingly difficult. The Orthodox community was neither large enough nor affluent enough, nor even sufficiently well-organized, to meet the needs and requirements of a major educational enterprise. The status of the seminary during its initial decade was extremely tenuous.

The death of Morais in 1897 brought the crisis almost to the point of disaster. Within a year the prestigious Sephardic Synagogue in New York, Shearith Israel, led an effort among Orthodox congregations to support only the newly created Rabbi Isaac Elchanan Yeshiva and thus repudiate its earlier agreement to back the Jewish

Theological Seminary. Having been categorically rejected by the major segment of the Orthodox community, the seminary leadership realized that they could ensure the seminary's future only by developing its own distinctive character.

The individual most personally responsible for the rescue of the seminary at this critical juncture was Cyrus Adler, a devoted disciple of Morais who was determined that his revered teacher's dream would not dissolve. On his own initiative, Adler enlisted the support of one of the foremost Jewish leaders and philanthropists of his day, Jacob H. Schiff. Schiff was actually a Reform Jew but also traced his roots to traditional sources in Germany, including a noted scholar who composed one of the better-known commentaries on the Talmud. Schiff persuaded several of his affluent German Reform brethren to respond to Adler's appeal, and he succeeded in raising more than half a million dollars among them to restructure the seminary and guarantee its financial future.

Their support, however, was not necessarily prompted by any personal enthusiasm for the ideals of this new movement. Instead, a penchant for paternalism convinced them that the flood of new Jewish immigrants from Eastern Europe would acculturate more easily, more quickly, and more completely through the efforts of the seminary than through any other vehicle. In their view the outlook and principles of Reform Judaism and its leadership were impossible to reconcile with the religious traditions and modes of living of these newcomers.

To succeed Sabbato Morais, the seminary board searched for a candidate who conceivably could communicate with his German patrons and his East European constituency. They found an outstanding prospect in the person of Solomon Schechter, whom they invited from England to become president of their institution in 1902. Schechter was a scholar of impeccable qualifications, but even more important for political purposes, a fortunate blend of both Jewish worlds. He was a native of Eastern Europe but an intellectual of Western experience and training. Schechter served for only thirteen years but at his death left an indelible and unsurpassed legacy of administrative expertise and scholarly attainment to Conservative Judaism. Much of the ideological foundation of the movement may be traced to his personal convictions and teachings.

Indeed, the very name Schechter chose to designate the national congregational body of Conservative Judaism in 1913 was the same as that of English Jewry, the United Synagogue. The United Synagogue is the counterpart of the Union of American Hebrew Congregations in Reform Judaism, and, as we shall discover later, of the Union of Orthodox Jewish Congregations in Orthodox Judaism. The original nucleus of sixteen congregations in the United Synagogue expanded steadily until it surpassed 830 affiliated synagogues, becoming the largest wing of American Judaism. Much of its growth undoubtedly derived from families of East European immigrants who rejected both the rigidities of Orthodoxy and the excesses of Reform.

The rabbinic arm of the Conservative movement originated in a seminary alumni association founded in 1901. In 1919, the alumni group evolved into the Rabbinical Assembly, opening its membership not only to graduates of the seminary, but to qualified applicants from other theological schools as well. The Rabbinical Assembly deliberates and articulates the position of Conservative Judaism on all matters of Jewish concern.

The Jewish Theological Seminary today is more than a preparatory academy for rabbis. It also includes a school for the training of cantors, a Teachers' Institute for instruction in education, a College of Jewish Studies for extension courses, and an enormous library with a vast collection of rare manuscripts. The seminary is the principal patron of the Jewish Museum in New York and has sponsored for many years an interesting, informative radio program, "The Eternal Light."

Like the Hebrew Union College-Jewish Institute of Religion, the seminary also supports campuses on the West Coast (the University of Judaism in Los Angeles) and in Israel at the American Student Center in Jerusalem, where many of its students spend an intensive year of study.

In spite of its emphasis on consensus as a standard for Jewish observance, the decision-making authority in the Conservative movement never did and still does not reside in its synagogues. It centers rather in the Law Committee of the Rabbinical Assembly. The United Synagogue does not exercise nearly the influence of its counterpart in the Reform movement, the Union of American

Hebrew Congregations. The Union exhibits far more leverage in directing the movement, not only with reference to its rabbinical schools, but also with reference to the formulation of policy and its execution. Conservative Judaism by contrast is a tightly knit structure at the highest echelons of leadership and is dominated by the directives of the Jewish Theological Seminary in New York City.

Organizationally, the Conservative movement addresses the needs and priorities of all its components, including the Ramah summer camps and Leadership Training Fellowship for young people, the National Academy for Adult Jewish Studies, the Women's League, and the Federation of Jewish Men's Clubs.

Conservative Judaism insists it is not simply another denomination in the fold of Jewish life. The movement claims to embrace the widest parameters of Judaism, conceiving itself as the mainstream of Jewish tradition which flows continuously in time and space with resurging vitality. It does not deny the existence of other movements in American Judaism, but relegates them to the category of tributaries that have always drifted to the left and right of normative Judaism, which it alone embodies.

Building on the dual assumptions that Jewish tradition must be preserved and conserved and that American Jewry must be directed to that course, the Conservative movement formulated not so much a theology as a technique. The technique attempted to achieve specific goals by devising concepts that would inspire them.

One such concept was "catholic Israel." The term was developed primarily by Solomon Schechter, but it may be traced much earlier to the notion of *k'lal Yisrael* ("the totality of Israel"). In reflecting upon the basic components of the Covenant, Conservative spokesmen contended that Reform had ignored both the centrality of Torah and the people Israel and had relegated Judaism to speculation about God and ethical principles. In similar fashion, Orthodoxy had fixed its vision on God and Torah but had ignored the needs of the Jewish people. Only Conservative Judaism, they argued, has restored the equal weight of all components in the Covenant. It staunchly upholds the centrality of God and Torah in Judaism, but it also assigns equivalent significance to the role of Israel as a people. It claims, therefore, that the Conservative movement has encouraged and supported the Zionist effort from the outset, and the condition of the Jewish people has always ranked among the highest priorities.

One exhibit submitted in evidence of this proposition is the explanation for including English in the traditional Hebrew service. English readings in the Conservative synagogue are not the consequence of theology or principle, but rather a realistic recognition that most Jews do not understand Hebrew, and many more do not even read it. The use of English thus enables a vast community of Jews to appreciate their heritage better. At the same time, Hebrew is emphasized both in worship and in education, because it is a major thread of continuity in Jewish life and Jewish history. It cannot be eliminated without dire consequences for the future vitality of the Jewish people. In this way, Conservative Judaism claims to meet the requirements both of Jewish history and of the Jewish people, or catholic Israel.

Another favorite concept in the Conservative vocabulary is "positive-historical Judaism." Originally, conceived by Zecharias Frankel in nineteenth-century Europe, the term refers essentially to the view that Judaism is the product of a long period of growth and evolution. That process, however, was not an uninterrupted series of developments. All currents of Judaism appear and reappear in different phases in all generations of Jewish experience. Every age builds upon the insights of its predecessors so that every innovation is the outcome of some earlier encounter with the tradition. It is impossible for anyone except God to create existence out of nothing. New forms are inevitably linked to old ones. As a major priority in Conservative Judaism, this notion implies respect for the Jewish past and an appreciation for the guiding principles of history. It further affirms a recognition of the fact that Judaism has changed continually over centuries of time and underscores the necessity of understanding the nature and causes of such change. The key to this understanding in the Conservative view is a focus upon the inner dynamism of Judaism. The Covenant has demonstrated an astounding capacity for flexibility; however, the tradition always retains an unmistakable thread of continuity. The positive-historical approach is thus an attempt to combine reverence for the past with equivalent respect for new realities. The formula for that blend is the product not of revolution but of evolution.

The evolutionary principle, however, contradicts the belief in divine revelation. One is the consequence of natural and gradual processes. The other requires a radical departure from the natural order. One way of coping with this dilemma has been to redefine the meaning of revelation in terms of rational criteria. Supporters of this view will regard revelation as a metaphor, a poetic expression, an inexplicable inspiration, or indirect guidance of supreme value.

Although Judaism may be evolutionary in character, the method of reshaping and remolding the contours of tradition cannot be left to sudden whim or spontaneous impulse. The task of preserving the past in the present is primarily the responsibility of the most learned and experienced scholars with ample consideration for the inclinations of their constituency as well as for the dictates of Jewish history. This methodology often includes reference to the concept of "vertical democracy." Vertical democracy is the recognition that proposals for change cannot be legislated by any single generation alone. Both past and future generations deserve to be consulted and allowed to vote, since the ultimate decision might modify the Covenant for all time. In assessing the merit of any change or innovation, consideration for the inclinations of the past is imperative. Ignoring the mandate would be an abrogation of responsibility

In its endorsement of the traditional theory of authority in Jewish life, leaders of the Conservative movement generally agree that decisions about Jewish law and observance properly belong to qualified scholars and specialists. In practice this means that lay people are discouraged and excluded from dealing with matters of ideology and basic policies. It also leads to an exceedingly heavy concentration of influence and decision-making authority in the seminary and its faculty instead of among congregational rabbis or educated lay leaders. This emphasis has enabled the more traditional segment of Conservative congregations to exercise considerably greater control over synagogue practices than they might ordinarily enjoy solely as a consequence of their numbers.

In spite of this theoretical ambivalence over the multiple loyalties to tradition and contemporary reality, the Conservative movement has parted company with the Jewish past in several categories. With rare exceptions, the Orthodox practice of separate seating for men and women has been abolished. The prayer book authorized by the United Synagogue eliminates the petition for the restoration of the sacrificial cult. The *musaf* ("additional") service on the Sabbath and festivals becomes a recollection of what the Jewish people did in the past instead of an anticipation of future observance. The reference to God as *m'chayeh hametim* ("He who brings life to the dead") emphasizes the creative power of God rather than His power of resurrection. The service also includes prayers in English.

Several Conservative synagogues include an organ for musical accompaniment, even though the melodies follow the traditional cantillation. In addition to the dominant ceremony of bar mitzvah for boys, the ceremony of bat mitzvah for girls is rapidly becoming a ritual feature. Confirmation, too, is increasingly more common. Even though Sabbath observance is closely aligned to the requirements of traditional practice, lay people are permitted to ride on the Sabbath for the purpose of attending the synagogue service. Provision is made for avoidable and unavoidable categories of work. Contrary to the strict dictates of Jewish law, a *cohen* ("descendent of the ancient priestly family") is permitted to marry a divorcee or a convert.

Part of the paradox in Conservative Judaism may stem from the fact that historically, both in America and in Europe, the movement developed by way of secession from the community of radical Reform. On the other hand, the vast majority of congregations which support the movement originally entered from the ranks of Orthodoxy. Intellectually, Conservative Judaism reflects a liberal inclination. Pragmatically, however, it is rooted deeply in attachments to the past. In contrast to Reform it seeks to embrace not only the essence of Judaism but the totality of tradition. Conversely, with reference to Orthodoxy, it fosters reverence not only for the contributions of Jewish tradition but for truth from all sources in all ages. Calibrating the balance between those two competing standards remains the principal challenge for Conservative Judaism.

3
Reconstructionist Judaism

Judaism functions only so long as it is co-extensive with the whole of the Jew's life.

Mordecai Kaplan (1881-)

One of the most prominent and productive of all Jewish theologians in the twentieth century has been Mordecai M. Kaplan. Regarded by many knowledgable observers of American Judaism as the most creative contemporary philosopher anywhere in the Jewish world, he is the founder of Reconstructionism, the end result of his own systematic analysis and assessment of the conditions of Jewish life in Western democracy. His views and those of the movement are therefore virtually interchangeable.

Kaplan came to America as a young boy from Lithuania in 1889 and pursued his formal education at the City College of New York, Columbia University, and the Jewish Theological Seminary of America. As a young rabbi, he served several Orthodox congregations in New York before he left the pulpit entirely in 1922 to organize the Society for the Advancement of Judaism. The Society evolved into a platform for circulating his own ideas and experiments in ritual and ceremony.

He also accepted a position at the Jewish Theological Seminary as professor of homiletics and Midrash which he held for more than forty years. In addition, he served as director of the seminary's Teachers' Institute. He taught at Columbia University Teachers College, at the former Graduate School for Jewish Social Work, and on many occasions at the Hebrew University in Jerusalem.

Kaplan has been a prolific author with scores of articles and a variety of books defining and defending his theory of Reconstructionism.

He began his extensive literary adventures in 1934 with the publication of *Judaism As A Civilization,* which provided a panorama of his views on Judaism and loosed a storm of controversy within Conservative Judaism. Kaplan perceived a need to face candidly and courageously a serious problem of disintegration in Jewish life. Essentially, he emphasized the necessity of reinterpreting Judaism to achieve better coherence with the requirements of rationalism and modernism in today's world. Neglect of that task, in his view, had contributed to alarming defections from the synagogue and Judaism. Jewish survival in America demanded therefore a radical "reconstruction" of belief and observance for contemporary Jews.

In 1934 Kaplan also initiated the widely read and popular periodical, *The Reconstructionist.* In 1940, he established the Reconstructionist Foundation, which promotes the goals of the movement and which publishes its own prayer books, textbooks, and related ideological tracts and manuals. For many years, Reconstructionism remained simply a school of thought, working with a wide range of existing Jewish institutions and leaving an intellectual impact on a diversity of people and programs. More recently, however, the movement organized the Reconstructionist Press and the Conference of Jewish Life and Thought, both of which are sponsored by the Jewish Reconstructionist Foundation. In 1968, the Foundation finally launched the Reconstructionist Rabbinical College in Philadelphia, which functions in a consortium arrangement with Temple University.

In Kaplan's view, religion is a social phenomenon, and an understanding of Judaism consequently begins with an understanding of the Jewish people. As an admirer of John Dewey, Kaplan assigns critical significance to the proper definition of terms, which consists largely of identifying their function, their affects, and effects.

The key to Kaplan's ideology is construing Judaism as a civilization, the character and components of which are determined by the Jewish people. The civilization of the Jewish people, however, is an evolutionary product of several stages whose common denominator is not belief, precept, or practice but the historical continuity of Israel, the people. Jewish religion exists to serve the needs of the Jewish people. The people do not exist to serve the needs of its faith. Judaism includes a history, law, language, literature, music, poetry, art, social organization, folkways, prevailing standards of conduct, social and spiritual ideals, and aesthetic values.

Like other civilizations, it also embraces a religion. Indeed, religion is inseparable from the fabric of Jewish civilization but still does not exhaust its significance. Both religious rituals and secular customs and habits are crucial in Jewish civilization as a total universe of symbols by which the Jew articulates his attachments to his Jewish community and culture. Hebrew is therefore essential to Jewish civilization, because it is the language of its literature and also provides a vital link of communication among Jews all over the world.

In Kaplan's formulation of Judaism, ritual practices should be classified more as *minhagim* ("customs" or "folkways") than as *mitzvoth* ("divine commandments"). "Folkways" are a better description of their purpose, because they reflect an idea or a mood that binds the individual to his or her people. They may facilitate communion with God, but they do not possess any magical powers. They simply revitalize the commitments of those who observe them and invigorate their lives with added meaning and significance.

Such observances are not mandatory as evidence of obedience to a preconceived absolute authority. Dietary customs, for example, may merit consideration to the extent that they invest the act of eating with a spiritual quality and add immeasurably to Jewish awareness at home. Since they are not immutable laws but optional folkways, it is not absolutely necessary to follow them in every meticulous detail or to sacrifice interaction with non-Jews because of them. Uncompromising compliance with dietary laws may be binding upon Orthodox Jews, but not upon those who reject the claim of divine origin for such regulations. They will instead stress the utility of ritual observance and the formulation of criteria for a selection process that will best enhance the quality of Jewish experience. Such an assessment may also include provision for new rituals and practices to reflect new values. For Reconstructionism, the ultimate aim is the quest for self-realization, as individuals and as a community, not a legal decree of infallible origin.

Ordinary religious observance is not the only method for strengthening attachments between individual Jews and their people. Kaplan suggests other intriguing options that serve the same end. One of them is the use of Jewish names. As evidence of a serious determination to live in two civilizations, he would advise a Jew to choose a first name that is distinctively Jewish and a family name more compatible with American culture.

Kaplan has also suggested a radical revision of the Hebrew calendar that currently derives from biblical genealogical tables based on the account of creation. Since that calendation is obviously invalid in light of current knowledge, he would base the origins of the religious calendar on the destruction of the Second Temple in the year 70 of the Common Era. That catastrophic event was clearly a turning point in Jewish history and was engraved indelibly on future generations until the restoration of the State of Israel in 1948.

As a civilization, Judaism embraces cherished values, interests, beliefs, and aspirations which accrued over the centuries of time and experience. The ideas and institutions it cherished most were elevated to the highest priority in order to preserve them. In religious language, that was a process of sanctification. Such customs and institutions became the *sancta* of the community, things that are special for the thoughts they evoke. Consequently, ceremonial objects, such as winecups, menorahs, Torah scrolls, or even the holy ark, were all decorated, embellished, and illuminated in a variety of ways as acts of endearment and attachment. Reverence for the sacred literature, the Torah, the Talmud, and the Midrash, reflects an equivalent reverence for certain ideas as sancta of the people.

Kaplan also emphasizes that Judaism should incorporate all components of a civilization, even if in its origins they were excluded. Sculpture, for example, was once a forbidden art form in Judaism because of its associations with idolatry. Since that danger no longer exists, sculpture should be encouraged and promoted as a legitimate and productive Jewish cultural pursuit. So, too, in Jewish worship, regardless of previous precedents, music, song, drama, and dance should be welcome assets for improving the aesthetic quality of prayer.

All these proposals for revision, Kaplan insists, require immediate deliberation. Collective decisions cannot wait for a legislative body of sufficient authority to evolve as the Orthodox require. The task is too urgent to permit any further delay for such a reassessment rooted in the rationale of Judaism as a civilization.

In general, the Reconstructionist approach might be described as naturalist in philosophy, liberal in theology, and nationalist in emphasis. The structure best suited to develop this approach and transpose it into reality is not the conventional synagogue, because that institution embraces only the religious compartment of Jewish life. The actual challenge of Jewish civilization requires a democratic Jewish community organization which would embrace the total diversity of Jewish views and institutions. The governing mechanism would consist of a coordinating community council to supervise and administer the operations of all its constituent agencies. Religious and educational activities would receive the highest priority since they touch the very heart of Jewish civilization. The remaining agencies, serving the social, cultural, recreational, and welfare needs of the people, would function on behalf of all. A major benefit of this consolidation process would be the elimination of waste, duplication, and inefficiency in the allocation of communal resources. The structure for such coordination at the local level could be amplified and expanded to regional and even national levels. Such a development would produce what Kaplan terms "the organic community.'

The Reconstructionists applaud the rise of the Jewish welfare funds and community councils as a welcome step in the gradual evolution of organic community. The current direction, however, even if completed, would remain inadequate, because the world of federation still does not encompass the religious and educational needs of the people or assign them the major emphasis they deserve. In the organic community, the school and synagogue occupy center stage in the unfolding drama of Jewish life.

Essentially, the Reconstructionist movement is promoting the end of congregational patterns of organization in favor of the *kehillah* ("community") structure of Central and Eastern Europe in earlier centuries. While in Europe the pattern was imposed upon Jews by external authorities in executing their segregationist policies, the new communal structure would be a voluntary association freely chosen as the most promising alternative for Jewish fulfillment and survival.

The closest analogy in American experience for the kehillah which Kaplan envisions is the model of the Roman Catholic Church with one major qualification. The Jewish kehillah would be thoroughly democratic in principle and practice and not nearly as authoritarian in character or hierarchical in structure. The prevailing theme in the

Jewish pattern would be "unity in diversity," which implies the widest possible latitude for all participating groups.

At the same time, the compensation for Jewish professionals and social service workers would be paid by the total Jewish community, not individual synagogues and agencies. Each school, too, would be supported by the kehillah rather than by individual congregations, which would enable students to deepen their loyalties to *K'lal Yisrael* ("the totality of Israel") rather than to particular synagogues or separate ideological segments of the Jewish spectrum. The organic community could thus become a forceful catalyst for Jewish unity. It would articulate and sustain the *we* feeling of the individual Jew, his sense of following the dominant direction for Jewish life and the Jewish people. That sense of sharing is the indispensable ingredient for safeguarding the vitality of Jewish civilization.

This persistent quest for unity in Kaplan's theology culminates in an actual revision of the concept of the covenant. The idea of covenant recedes from the spotlight of Jewish values and functions instead as another folkway or "sanctum" in Kaplan's collection. Covenant, in his view, is actually an instrument for initiating new epochs in Jewish experience. There have been several such covenants in history, beginning with Abraham, continuing with Moses at Sinai, the reformation under Josiah, the proclamations of Ezra and Nehemiah, the revolt of the Hasmoneans, and continuing far beyond into more recent times with the revolt of the Warsaw ghetto and the establishment and defense of modern Israel.

Current realities and future requirements persuade Kaplan of the need for a covenant assembly to be held in Jerusalem to which every faction of world Jewry would be invited. The agenda would begin with a recognition that the restoration of the Jewish state launches a new stage in Jewish history. It would continue with the formulation of a covenant that would establish the foundation for a transnational Jewish community, rooted in Israel but with branches extending to every corner of the globe. Although every Jew would proclaim his political allegiance to the country in which he lived, the covenant would bind him in moral and spiritual fidelity to all his people all over the world. It should be emphasized that the Covenant most frequently associated with Judaism also implies the same attachments and responsibilities.

In its theology Reconstructionism is in many ways a much further departure from the ordinary norms than the early formulations of Reform Judaism. The focus of Jewish faith is salvation, which Kaplan defines as the "progressive perfection of the human personality and the establishment of a free, just, and cooperative social order" (Kaplan, *Future of the American Jew,* 1957, p. xvii). This quest for salvation is a continuous thread in every developing stage of Jewish tradition. It surfaces in different forms, but the message remains the same. Even by Kaplan's rational criteria, the truth of salvation is still impossible to demonstrate by empirical experience. It is a matter of faith, but nonetheless imperative, because without such belief a person is likely to despair entirely of improving his own life and that of future generations. Kaplan insists that there are resources in the world and in human nature that will facilitate human effort and hasten the dawn of that better tomorrow which promises freedom, justice, and equality for all. In the Reconstructionist lexicon, God is therefore the "power that makes for salvation" (Kaplan, *Judaism As A Civilization,* 1957, p. 317). Without God the striving toward perfection would be a cosmic absurdity. God is the assurance that the human struggle for fulfillment can succeed.

Reconstructionism classifies as revelation any knowledge which people require in order to attain salvation regardless of its source. The introduction to its prayer book clearly states that "not God revealed the Torah to Israel, but the Torah revealed God to Israel" (*Sabbath Prayer Book,* p. xxv). The lesson is that what a person understands about God or any other reality is the result of patient, persistent searching and not a miraculous intervention from a supernatural source. The Bible therefore is the product of man's communication with God rather than of God's communication with man.

In Kaplan's system, evil is comparable to darkness. Just as light can eliminate the darkness, so goodness can overcome evil. Evil is simply the absence of good, even as darkness is the absence of light. The theory also implies an existential challenge. The extent to which goodness prevails depends upon the willingness and incentive of people to labor on its behalf. Man may indeed become an active partner with God in the process of perfecting the world.

This naturalistic view of reality and the universe poses serious questions about the significance of prayer in its ordinary context.

For a Reconstructionist, prayer is not so much a matter of summoning God as it is a matter of summoning the godly within one's self and attempting to meet its requirements, however difficult. Prayer is a subjective experience, a self-searching, a personal spiritual inventory of strengths and weaknesses, and a determined effort to achieve harmony and balance with the rhythms of life. It is an opportunity as well to articulate the deepest longings and aspirations, to link personal hopes with the ultimate vision of the community, a stimulus in the active pursuit of fulfillment or salvation.

Like the Reform movement, and to some extent like Conservative Judaism as well, Reconstructionism objects to the outmoded passages of the traditional prayer book. Instead of merely modifying the wording or syntax of such portions as the Conservative movement did, the Reconstructionists followed the lead of Reform Judaism by eliminating them entirely. References to the sacrificial cult, the rebuilding of the Temple, or the priestly prerogatives are deleted completely. Like the Conservative prayer book, however, the Reconstructionist liturgy retains a tribute to the spiritual quality of absolute devotion that accompanied the ancient sacrificial cult.

One of the most intriguing distinctions of Reconstructionist ideology is the elimination of the historic concept of Israel as the "chosen people," although many modern Reconstructionists have expressed misgivings about the movement's rejection of the concept of *election*. Kaplan rejected this doctrine, because he viewed it as the vestige of a supernatural emphasis in Judaism. He explained it as a device which people probably invented to maintain their own self-esteem in the face of blatant hostility toward Jews for centuries. In a society that flourishes on democratic ideals, the notion of "chosenness" conveys a climate of superiority wholly inappropriate and superfluous. Kaplan concedes that the intent of the election of Israel was to summon the Jewish people to a life of service as models of moral excellence, but he still insists it touches too closely the realm of moral arrogance. He substitutes instead the idea of vocation, contending that all peoples are endowed with special competence or potential in a wide range of human disciplines. None is better than any other. Each is simply different from all others. Every community is or can be a contributor to human progess.

Many components of Reconstructionism appeal not only to its for-

4
Orthodox Judaism

Since all revelation is divine involvement with men, and since all involvement is affirmation of the things God desires, revelation and law are inseparable. The encounter at Sinai revealed God as well as His law to Israel.

Eliezer Berkovitz (1900–)

A popular impression of Orthodox Judaism assumes that it is a monolithic movement, that all Orthodox Jews believe and practice the same faith. That premise is entirely false. Orthodoxy spans a range of complexity at least as varied as that of any other sector of American Judaism.

All segments of the Orthodox community subscribe to the proposition that the supreme binding force in Jewish life is *Halakah* ("Jewish law"). The difficulty with that proposition and the source of dispute in Orthodox ranks is the issue of legitimate authority in both legislating and interpreting Halakah. Tradition stipulates that such authority rests with the *G'dolim* ("leaders"); but the Orthodox factions have not been able to agree on the requirements of such leadership. Hence the fragmentation of ideology and observance.

Despite this division within the fold, American Orthodoxy has begun to distinguish itself institutionally, to develop its own organizational structure, and to promote its own cause as a movement rather than to serve simply as a voice for all Jews. This process has been the consequence of several decades of gradual development. The march to structural maturity began with the appeal to thousands of the East European immigrants who transformed the religious landscape of American Jewry by the end of the nineteenth century.

Most of the new arrivals from Eastern Europe were complete strangers to the non-Jewish world. They spoke Yiddish and came from isolated villages in lands quarantined exclusively for Jewish settlement. They were poor, uncultured, and totally lacking in worldly knowledge, although many were often well trained in the classics of Hebrew religious literature such as the Bible, Talmud, and Mishnah. They came to America knowing only one brand of Judaism, Orthodoxy, for religious liberalism of any kind by their standards was sacrilegious. Many of the more knowledgeable and observant newcomers found the American setting wholly incompatible with their religious training and value scheme. They reflected with yearning and regret on the spiritual autonomy they had enjoyed in their native countries, where the synagogue and study hall had dictated proper standards of truth and conduct. They also longed for a community in which the celebration of holy days and festivals, personal milestones, and special occasions all commanded universal observance without the competing distractions of a non-Jewish environment. Adjustment to America for these immigrants was exceedingly difficult, and neither Reform nor Conservative Judaism could offer them adequate alternatives.

At the same time, it was self-evident that they would never be able to duplicate the patterns of the old country in this new world. Instead, they proceeded to shape their tradition in a different mold, sacrificing as little of its content as they possibly could. One of the first projects in this scheme was the establishment of a *yeshiva* ("school for Talmudic studies") on the Lower East Side of New York in 1896. The Isaac Elchanan Yeshiva was named for the great Talmudic sage of Kovno, Lithuania, Rabbi Isaac Elchanan. It was modeled on European prototypes, which explains why most of its curriculum was originally designed for the preparation of students for *semicha* ("ordination") and their training as *talmidei chachamim* ("learned scholars").

In 1906 the student body petitioned the faculty to expand the curriculum to include secular studies. After considerable debate and deliberation, the request was granted, and the Yeshiva embarked on a radical departure from its East European counterpart. Higher education at the Yeshiva would now enable observant Jews to combine their program for professional training with considerable competence in Talmudic studies.

This initial modification was only the opening stage in a long series of accommodations that would broaden significantly the conceptual boundaries of Orthodox Judaism. In 1915 under the leadership of its president, Dr. Bernard Revel, the Yeshiva organized a preparatory school on the Lower East Side, the Yeshiva Etz Chaim, which also combined programs of secular and Jewish learning. In 1921, the Yeshiva absorbed the Mizrachi Teachers Training School as one of its divisions.

The most decisive turning point for this citadel of Orthodox Jewish learning occurred, however, in 1928 when Dr. Revel succeeded in creating a liberal arts college independent of the theological school and invested with the authority to grant baccalaureate degrees. This revolutionary development enabled young Orthodox Jews to obtain a competitive undergraduate education without comprising the rigorous requirements of Jewish studies. This consolidation of secular and religious learning was totally unprecedented as a pattern in Jewish life.

After Dr. Revel's death, his successor, Dr. Samuel Belkin, secured accreditation for Yeshiva College in 1943 as a full university with the right to confer advanced degrees, including doctorates. Yeshiva University now operates as a nonsectarian institution with seven graduate schools and five undergraduate schools on four campuses in the Bronx and Manhattan, as well as an affiliated teachers' college in Los Angeles.

The growth of Yeshiva University reflected in many ways the growth and emerging maturity of Orthodox Judaism in America. Several Orthodox spokesmen recognized the need for a unified, representative body to articulate the principles and aspirations which it cherished most. Responding to that need, however, defied the efforts of the best minds and hearts of Orthodox Jews for several reasons.

The complexity of background among Orthodox Jews was astounding. The community included immigrants from Russia, Poland, Rumania, Lithuania, Galicia, Austria, and Hungary, as well as a generous supply of faithful followers from Western Europe. The ideological spectrum was even more complex than the ethnic composition. Individual synagogues were barely able to sustain themselves, far less support the superstructure of a national movement. Furthermore, the relative isolation and autonomy they had inherited from the countries whence they came seriously hampered their ability to cope with democratic procedures of compromise and cooperation.

In spite of all these obstacles, a determined nucleus of native Orthodox Jewish leaders labored incessantly and finally secured enough support in 1898 to launch a national body of Orthodox congregations. Called the Union of Orthodox Congregations, it demonstrated from the outset a disposition to reconcile the Orthodoxy of Eastern Europe with the rapidly changing character of American society.

As part of its current agenda, the supervision of *kashruth* (''dietary laws'') is under the direction of the rabbinical arm of the Union, the Rabbinical Council of America. Consumers are protected from the increased costs of such disposition and preparation of foods by an agreement with the manufacturers to absorb the added expense themselves. While the six-day work week was still the prevailing norm, the Union also sponsored a Jewish Sabbath Alliance which operated an employment bureau to locate jobs that would allow Sabbath observance for Jewish workers.

Like its counterparts in the Reform and Conservative movements, the Union of Orthodox Congregations promotes its own projects and programs in education, most of them in cooperation with Yeshiva University. It, too, has sponsored its own women's branch, youth movement, and even the Association of Orthodox Jewish Scientists.

The Union is clearly the most articulate and respected voice of American Orthodoxy. Although it includes only a fraction of the nearly seventeen hundred Orthodox congregations in the country, many if not most of the largest and wealthiest are affiliated as active constituents and supporters.

Corresponding to the multiplicity of congregational bodies in Orthodox Judaism is the proliferation of rabbinic organizations. The wide differences in background and training among Orthodox rabbis account in large measure for the variations in thought and practice. The oldest association of all is the *Aggudath Ha-Ravvanim*, also known as the Union of Orthodox Rabbis of the United States and Canada. It was organized in 1902 with an original membership of fifty rabbis, all of whom were born and educated in Eastern Europe.

One of its most prominent spokesmen and administrators was Israel Rosenberg, a distinguished Orthodox rabbi and founder of the Isaac Elchanan Yeshiva. Among its projects was the creation of the *Ezrath Torah* ("Aid to Torah") Fund which has provided aid to needy rabbis, scholars, and *yeshivot* ("Talmud schools") in Eastern Europe. It also sponsored the *Vaad Hatzala* "(Committee for Rescue") during World War II which saved hundreds of sages and scholars from destruction and transferred many of their academies to Palestine and America. The organization tends to favor stringent interpretation of Jewish law and, in recent years, has declined considerably in status and influence.

Several younger rabbinic groups have captured a growing segment of the observant Orthodox community. One of these groups is the Rabbinical Council of America (RCA), formed in 1930 as the result of a merger between the Rabbinical Alumni Association of the Isaac Elchanan Yeshiva and the Rabbinical Council of the Union of Orthodox Jewish Congregations (UOJC). In 1942 the RCA also admitted into its membership the Rabbinical Association of the Hebrew Theological College in Chicago, and later, the graduates of Ner Israel Rabbinical College in Baltimore. In addition, the RCA will welcome qualified candidates whose ordination was supervised by "proper" authorities. It presently serves as the rabbinical arm of the UOJC.

The RCA is unquestionably the largest and most effective Orthodox rabbinical body with a membership that now surpasses eight hundred men. It publishes an outstanding periodical, *Tradition*, a legal journal in Hebrew, *HaDorom*, and a newsletter, "The RCA Record." In recent years it has also established a *Bet Din* ("rabbinic court") to deliberate and decide complex issues of Halakah.

On the periphery of the rabbinic spectrum in Orthodoxy are associations such as the Rabbinical Alliance of America, known for its austere ideology, and the Central Rabbinical Congress, which consists almost exclusively of Hassidic rabbis. The Union of Orthodox Rabbis and the RCA remain the major organizations speaking for Orthodoxy in the United States.

Ideologically, it is easier to understand Orthodox Judaism in terms of the concepts which its theological schools teach than those which its followers practice. Affiliation with an Orthodox synagogue is not necessarily evidence of commitment to its principles. Jews will join or continue membership in the most traditional of synagogues for family ties, nostalgia, or sometimes guilt, as well as for reasons of conviction. Some Orthodox congregations cope with the enigma of a formal affirmation of traditional practice which few members follow except the rabbi.

Theoretically, the standards for Orthodox Jewish practice are clearly defined in the *Shulkan Aruch* (1657), the traditional code of Jewish law. The reality, however, is far more complex, because a "nonobservant Orthodox Jew" is a contradiction in terms. Traditional observance is the necessary prerequisite for acceptance as an Orthodox Jew. Disregard for this requirement is a repudiation of the central theses of Orthodox thought.

Orthodox Judaism proceeds from the premise that the Covenant in its entirety is the product of divine revelation. The Covenant in this context includes not only the Bible (Written Law) and subsequent rabbinic tradition (Oral Law), but the codification of those teachings in the *Shulkan Aruch* and its commentaries, as well as decisions by respected rabbinic authorities based on interpretations from those sources. In more recent times, this appeal to authenticity through traditional sources has persuaded portions of the Orthodox community to define its theological stance as "Torah-true" Judaism. They perceive themselves as guardians of the Torah and its commandments with the duty to preserve them and follow them regardless of changing times or circumstances.

The supreme standard for maintaining the Covenant in Orthodoxy is Halakah. The ultimate criterion for human conduct is the revealed will of God as disclosed in Halakah, and not in the constant fluctuation of contemporary values and mores. This assertion, however, poses a fundamental dilemma between the requirements of observance and the status of individual Jews. On the one hand, Orthodox authorities refuse to include in their domain any Jew who defies the dictates of Jewish law. On the other hand, Jewish law itself stipulates that any person born of a Jewish mother is a Jew regardless of the quality of his observance. The Orthodox establishment has found it difficult, if not impossible, to resolve this dilemma and find a way of respecting the larger portion of American Jewry that no longer subscribes to Halakah. Some Orthodox authorities favor a policy of withdrawal from the majority to avoid an implicit recognition of illegitimate ideologies. Others have promoted a more conciliatory approach for the purpose of preserving Jewish unity regardless of theological debates.

A sizeable segment of the modern Orthodox movement is under severe attack for supposedly condoning deviations from strict Halakic standards in order to attract nonobservant Jews. At the same time, other sectors of Orthodoxy complain about the irrational rigidity of the movement which refuses to acknowledge and address the inevitable consequences of emancipation and enlightenment and the enormous impact of the rise of the State of Israel. They charge that Orthodoxy has been content to condemn its opposition instead of dealing constructively with new, historic realities.

One of the most prominent world spokesmen for Orthodoxy is Rabbi Joseph Soloveitchik, who had the distinction of being invited in 1960 to become the Ashkenazic Chief Rabbi of Israel but declined. Dr. Soloveitchik proposes to resolve the dilemma by explaining Halakah as a system of ultimate ideals which no disciple can ever observe in its totality. He maintains that Halakah presents a prescription for the details of conduct in the ideal life, conditioned by the recognition that ordinary mortals cannot achieve a utopian state of existence. Short of attaining perfection, however, the observant Jew may still strive to achieve distinction by clinging as closely as he can to the dictates of Halakah. A serious Jew should investigate and examine not only the functional components of Jewish law, but also the most abstract and theoretical aspects. As Rabbi Soloveitchik observes, the truly devoted Jew is like the mathematician who realizes that no existing geometric figure perfectly reflects its theoretical model, but understands also that such models provide the truths by which scientists in several disciplines may derive the laws they require in their respective fields. Similarly, Halakah establishes the norms of fulfilling the Covenant to which all Jews should aspire.

Orthodox Judaism is still in search of a systematic theology which can accommodate traditional claims to the discoveries of modern science and historic scholarship. An even more fundamental challenge is the task of constructing a theory of revelation that would command the respect of competing intellectual disciplines. Some would deemphasize the supernatural quality of divine disclosures and stress the subjective human response to the teachings of tradition. Whether or not sufficient latitude exists in the Orthodox community to meet this test remains an open question. More than a few leading Orthodox authorities have demonstrated very clearly their adamant opposition to any compromises with the doctrine that divine revelation consists of direct communication of content from God to man.

Even more perplexing are the implications of the emphasis in Orthodoxy on the supreme authority of Halakah. Such an arbitrary standard of judgment is difficult to reconcile in a democratic society with a cultural affinity for pluralism and the freedom of individual choice. In addition, while Orthodoxy assigns ultimate allegiance to Halakah, Orthodox rabbis themselves cannot agree on what Halakah requires on any particular issue. Periodic efforts to establish a central authority have failed completely. Even the occasional summons to revive the ancient Sanhedrin evokes fierce controversy in the ranks of the Orthodox establishment. It has thus far been a futile enterprise even to organize a loose structure of representative components within Orthodox Judaism just to facilitate communication among its various segments.

One strand of Orthodoxy which differs considerably in its history and observance from the usual pattern of traditional Judaism is the small but diverse world of Hasidism. Hasidism is a movement that originated in the southeast section of Poland in the eighteenth century under the initial leadership and inspiration of Israel ben Eleizer, more widely known as the *Baal Shem Tov* (''Master of the Good Name'') or by the abbreviated name ''Besht.'' The movement emphasized that the path of service to God began with inner commitment and joyful awareness of the Creator in nature and human experience. It attached the highest priority to emotional exultation and acceptance of the most insignificant tasks of life as divine challenges. Study and learning were not irrelevant, but they were insufficient without the basic components of sincerity and enthusiasm.

Hasidism eventually faltered. The forms changed, but the initial spirit vanished. The leaders formed dynasties, and the sons succeeded by inheritance to their fathers' authority. They served essentially as absolute rulers of their communities. The fatal flaw of

Hasidism ultimately was its failure to resist successfully the crippling weakness of the very formalization and ritualization it first opposed in the Jewish establishment. Hasidic groups still exist in America, but they are only distantly related to the initial impulse which inspired them. Most of them are extremely strict in their observance of Jewish law and display little tolerance for Jews who reject their standards.

The traditions, customs, dress, and practices of the Hasidim pervaded every aspect of their daily lives and still do. Under the guidance of their religious leaders, they cultivate a separate, isolated existence much like the Amish or Mennonite movements in the Christian communities of America. In contrast to the inclination of earlier waves of Jewish immigrants, the Hasidim deliberately seek to perpetuate all the distinctive practices, norms, and values they inherited from their lands of origin. They have never sought any integration with American culture, but are in fact determined to resist it. They cherish American society primarily because it ensures them the freedom to maintain their isolation.

Hasidim are distinctive by their appearance. The men wear beards. Male children wear *peyot* ("long earlocks of hair") and married women shave their natural hair and wear *sheitels* ("wigs"). On the Sabbath and special festivals, a majority of men dress in caftans, fur hats, white stockings and black slippers. The children are sent to their own private religious schools, where boys and girls attend separate facilities. The curriculum includes only that secular education the state requires, although some parents resent even such a minimum and deem it an exercise in heresy.

The entire community bans all expressions of popular culture, including mixed dancing, radio, television, and contemporary secular literature. They still attach a high priority to the element of joy in the performance of religious duties, although it is often difficult to detect and is restricted to a relatively narrow range of permissible activities, such as singing and storytelling on the Sabbath and holidays, games and parodies on Purim, or ordinary athletics during leisure hours.

The Hasidim introduced into American Orthodoxy the category of *glatt kosher* ("perfectly kosher") products. Such products are suitable for purchase and consumption only if they meet the requirements of authorities whose competence is approved by the leader. A number of Hasidic communities have also developed *shatnez* laboratories for the purpose of testing fabrics to determine whether or not they contain mixtures of wool and linen, which are prohibited by biblical law (Lev. 19:19; Deut. 22:11).

Numerous Hasidic groups have established settlements in Israel, but a few consider the restoration of Jewish sovereignty a profanation of God's name. Their denunciation of the Jewish state rests upon the traditional claim that the ingathering of the Jewish people to their ancient homeland could occur only in the historical framework of the Messianic Age as an act of God, not of man. Since Zionism and modern Jewish nationalism are the products of human agencies and not divine ones, many Hasidim contend that the consequences are not only invalid but contemptible as well.

In fact, the Hasidic leader known as the Satmar Rebbe, Rabbi Joel Teitelbaum, proclaims that the Holocaust was a divine punishment for the sin of Zionism and the movement to establish a Jewish state. In Israel, his disciples speak Yiddish, not Hebrew; the latter is reserved exclusively as a sacred language. They even align themselves with the small but vociferous extremist Orthodox sect in Jerusalem called *Neturei Katra* (''Guardians of the City''), which has defied the right of the Israeli government to rule in Jerusalem or anywhere else in the Holy Land.

The most visible and energetic Hasidic sect in America are the followers of the Lubavitcher Rebbe. In many respects, the Lubavitcher movement is the least sectarian of Orthodox groups, although in doctrinal purity it is the most faithful to the precepts of its founders. It ranks as well among the most intellectually sophisticated and effectively organized segments of Hasidic Jewry.

The Lubavitcher sect does not acknowledge political or religious divisions within Judaism. It has refused to register formally with any particular organization or institution. It distinguishes only between two categories of Jews—those who already are devout and fully observant Lubavitcher Jews and those who are not but could be. Lubavitcher emissaries are convinced that a divine spark resides in every human person which awaits only the necessary firebrand to burst into an inexhaustible flame. The longest journey, they emphasize, begins with the smallest step; the path to complete piety begins with the first mitzvah. Every Jew is a sacred creature even though the criteria of sanctity belong to the Lubavitcher movement alone.

While the Hasidic mold of living is a rare phenomenon among American Jews, its philosophy and ideology have contributed significantly to the climate of Jewish life and religion in America. It has shaped a meaningful portion of contemporary Jewish thought, particularly in the work of Martin Buber (1878–1965) who reflected one of its major themes in his formulation of the I-Thou concept of human interaction with God and the universe. Buber echoed fundamental precepts of Hasidism in proclaiming that the shortest road from man to God leads through humanity, and that the goal of all human striving must be the unity of all people in unity with God. For Buber and Hasidism that formula was the way to redemption and the process for bringing about the Messianic Age.

An Hasidic flavor is also evident in the phenomenon of *chavurot* ("fellowships") in which individuals with similar spiritual inclinations will join together to build a sense of community among themselves while retaining their own unique identity. It may be evident, too, among young people and adults in summer camps or synagogues who have experimented with new worship forms and patterns. Many have discovered that through special music and creative interaction with each other they can heighten their own self-awareness and their appreciation for everyone else. That recognition is rooted in the Hasidic faith that there is a God within ourselves and the world Whom we can experience if we are receptive. The basic prerequisite is not the intellectual argument but the emotional reality.

The Hasidim discovered God by feeling His presence continuously in every ordinary act. That message and yearning have found their way into the realm of general philosophy and theology and pose a formidable challenge to the more conventional intellectual disciplines. In terms of universal impact, therefore, Hasidism remains a significant contribution to religion, to Judaism as a whole, and to Orthodoxy in particular.

In more recent times Orthodox Judaism in general seems to have entered a period of revival and regeneration. One reason may be that when Jews seek to return to Judaism and to rejoin the Covenant, they perceive its requirements as Orthodoxy defines them. They see the Orthodox way as the authentic version of what Judaism has always been. It most closely resembles for them the enduring tradition they seek to recapture. Orthodoxy seems to exhibit none of the confusion, the vacillation, or potentially fatal compromises of Conservative or Reform Judaism. The major asset of Orthodoxy is its persistent claim to exclusive legitimacy for the observance of Judaism and a determination to persuade its followers that it alone reflects the eternal verities of Jewish tradition.

Epilogue

As the idea of a common humanity forms its beginning, so Judaism will attain its final goal only in a divine covenant comprising all humanity.

Kaufmann Kohler (1841–1926)

The attempt to define the meaning and significance of the Covenant in Judaism for any given generation is an extremely risky venture. Even if it reflects the prevailing trends of the time, it is still subject to change. How future events and circumstances will alter the analysis we have just completed belongs entirely in the realm of speculation. It would be foolish to contend that previous patterns of change are entirely useless in forecasting future ones, but it would also be futile to chart precisely the course which Jewish life will follow.

We may at best cite a range of current variables which will perhaps contribute to inevitable changes without dwelling on the particular details of those shifts in direction. Indeed, an assessment of the present condition is wholly inadequate without anticipating such agents of change.

One of these variables is the increasingly blurred distinctions among the major movements in American Judaism. A generation ago or more, the differences between one segment and another in American Jewry were much more clearly defined. The boundaries between such movements as Orthodox, Conservative, Reform, and Reconstructionist Judaism were virtually unmistakable. A knowledgeable observer could identify the category to which any synagogue belonged by analyzing its ritual. An Orthodox synagogue never permitted mixed seating or musical accompaniment. Conservative synagogues never allowed women to lead the congregation in worship. Reform temples never provided men with headcoverings or *taletim* (''prayer shawls'') for public prayer. Such distinctions no longer prevail. Synagogues that call themselves Orthodox provide a section of their sanctuary for mixed seating. The Conservative movement is currently debating the ordination of women into the rabbinate. An increasing number of Reform Jews are worshipping with covered heads and are even seriously considering the observance of *kashruth* (''dietary laws'').

Many young people find the distinctions between the movements increasingly less significant, if not trivial. They perceive themselves not so much in terms of being Orthodox, Conservative, Reform, or Reconstructionist Jews, but of being steadfast Jews or ''occasional'' Jews. Either they are serious about the regularity of their Jewish commitment and observance or they reserve such allegiance to special holidays or particular milestones in their personal lives. Their loyalty to Judaism is more a matter of individual performance than of adherence to institutions.

Coupled with the fact that similarities among Jews have always transcended their differences, these increasingly hazy distinctions between the major movements may signal substantial revision in the organizational apparatus of American Judaism in the future. The fluid quality of religious behavior among American Jews may produce more than a modest realignment of major forces in the synagogue community.

Another variable of enormous magnitude is the increasing incidence of mixed marriage. Estimates of marital unions between Jews and non-Jews now range as high as 40 percent. Despite the efforts to stem the tide of such matches, the trend is likely to continue if not accelerate, given the mobility and openness of American society. The principal issue may no longer be one of how to prevent it but of how to cope with it.

The most reliable studies suggest that in the vast majority of cases in which the non-Jewish spouse converts to Judaism, the children of such marriages are reared as Jews. More surprisingly, in a significant number of cases where the non-Jewish spouse does not convert, the children are nonetheless still raised in a religious atmosphere in which Judaism dominates. That pattern reflects the reality at least in America. Elsewhere, especially in Europe, where national cultures are less pluralistic and less receptive to ethnic distinctions, the prospects may not be as promising. There the temptation for Jews to absorb the majority position is far more compelling. In those countries, Jewish solidarity often wavers and weakens; and Jewish communities drop sharply in their level of activity and visibility.

In any event, whatever the outcome of mixed marriage may be in terms of conversion, its current phenomenal growth will inevitably alter the current patterns of Jewish belief and practice. If Judaism has forever been shaped and guided by the cultural conditioning of Jews who maintained it, the contours of Judaism in America will inevitably change to reflect the experience of many people who became Jews by choice and not by birth. Perceptions about Jewish history, Jewish holidays, and life cycle ceremonies will obviously be different for those individuals without any Jewish ancestors than for those with such roots. Educational assumptions and curricula cannot be the same for children with one set of grandparents who are Jewish and another who are not. Clearly, the rapidly growing incidence of conversion will accentuate the significance of *am'cha* ("peoplehood") as a spiritual entity rather than an ethnic community.

Perhaps even more important to the future configuration of the Covenant than intermarriage and assimilation is the alarmingly low birth rate among American Jews. Whether the explanation may be attributed to greater sexual freedom, fewer and later marriages, more divorces, or lower fertility, the trend implies a sharply declining Jewish population in the future. Quantity may not be as crucial as quality, but certain basic components of community well-being, such as education, social services for youth, for families, and the elderly, defense agencies, support for Israel, and cultural vitality, all depend upon a critical mass in numbers. It may not require six million Jews to ensure a spiritual vitality in America, but it will not be sustained by half that number or less. Essential operations of religious and cultural institutions require certain minimal levels of funding and active participation, and those levels in turn depend upon a crucial base of constituents. The closing of synagogues in smaller communities across the country for lack of adequate memberships demonstrates the malady brought on by demographic change.

Anti-Semitism, too, is an unpredictable but perennial variable. It may rise or fall as a social barometer of political and economic tranquility, but it constantly simmers beneath the surface of any Jewish religious agenda. It is almost a universal axiom that nothing in their experience binds Jews more closely together than external threats to their safety and security, but at the same time meeting those threats drains them of enormous time and energy which could otherwise be channeled into more productive avenues of religious experience. Regrettably, Jews worry less about the number of students in Jewish schools than about the number of anti-Semites in the world. They worry less about the level of Jewish education among adults than about the level of hostility among Jewish hatemongers. What will really make a difference for American Jews, which many have thus far failed to acknowledge, is what they do to revitalize their faith and strengthen their ties to each other, not what the rest of the world believes or thinks or does about them.

Recent surveys reveal that anti-Semitism and other forms of racial and religious bigotry remain a virulent social disease. It is not a question of ignoring completely the resurgence of anti-Semitism in too many places. That development requires constant surveillance. It is rather a matter of priorities, a question of solemn resolve and determination that Jewish life will be so vigorous and vibrant that it will weather the storm of any social turmoil, however severe or relentless. Reverence for the Covenant will accomplish far more than preoccupation with anti-Semites.

The success of that effort hinges in turn on still another variable, the quality and character of Jewish leadership. The last survivors of the earlier immigrant population are rapidly passing on. The highest echelons of Jewish leadership are no longer filled, as they were some years ago, by rabbis, judges, and other spiritual and intellectual leaders whom the older generation had followed. Since the establishment of the State of Israel, world Jewry is no longer guided by leaders like Justice Louis D. Brandeis, Justice Felix Frankfurter, Rabbi Abba Hillel Silver, or Rabbi Stephen S. Wise. The seats of influence and decision making are now occupied by the leading figures of Israeli politics.

In America, the leadership of the Jewish community has passed to successful and wealthy business people with wholly different commitments and interests than their more intellectual predecessors. The new leaders derive their credibility from their capacity to raise huge sums needed by Israel and other Jewish communities in distress; these are leaders who enjoy easy access to government figures and policymakers. Yet by a stroke of irony, even this generation of leaders is fading from power. Their own children have increasingly retreated from family businesses and the pursuit of material well-being in favor of careers in law, medicine, university teaching, research, the arts, and other intellectual pursuits. They focus more often on a universalist and secular agenda, not a Judaic one. Unlike their parents and grandparents, the new generation of articulate Jewish spokesmen do not share the memories and experiences of recent climactic turning points in Jewish history. For most of them the Holocaust is an event of the distant past; for many it is even difficult to remember a world in which there never was a Jewish state.

Although many young Jews have become active in Jewish affairs, these generational changes emotionally and professionally raise serious questions about the future of Jewish leadership and the centrality of spiritual ideals as the essence of Judaism. Perpetuating the Covenant for the future may require a more concerted effort to recruit a considerably larger sample of outstanding, well-educated Jews in Jewish communal life than ever before.

By far the most critical variable of all in determining the future form and content of Judaism in America is the impact of Israel. For Jews in the Diaspora, Israel has served variously as a source of identity, peoplehood, pride, and dignity, as a potential haven or a spiritual center, and for many others, as a surrogate for Judaism, if not a secular religion. For Israel, Jews in America and in other Western democracies represent an irreplaceable source of economic, moral, and political support. They are also the most fertile prospects for future immigration as well as for intellectual, scientific, and technological assistance. Israel and Diaspora Jewry, especially American Jewry, are mutually dependent. Each is essential to the other, and each exerts a reciprocal influence and cultural pull on the other.

At the same time, the two communities are not without their disagreements. Some observers attribute those differences and difficulties to problems in "communications." In most instances, however, they do not entail problems of language; rather they reflect important differences on basic issues of ideology. Frequently, those rifts evolve out of conflicting expectations about the goals and purposes of a Jewish state. For many American Jews, the policies of a Jewish state cannot be divorced from the moral mandate of Jewish faith. For many Israelis, the requirements of nationhood and those of Judaism are entirely separate. And in the eyes of many, both in Israel and the Diaspora, never the twain shall meet.

Few will challenge the proposition that Israel will continue to play a central role in Jewish life. The real question is whether or not that role will exhaust all other indigenous creative ventures within American Jewry. Certainly the centrality of Israel is paramount in providing physical and spiritual insurance for Jews in the Diaspora, and in serving as an immediate haven for those communities faced with a precarious existence which results from external threats or internal disintegration. It also serves as the world center to preserve, embody, and renew Jewish traditions and values, to preserve Jewish history, and to infuse new life into Jewish culture. It is the central address for Jewish existence in the world today which binds all Jews into a single community. The fundamental issue is whether that community is compatible with the religious dimensions of the Covenant from which most Jews derive their inspiration as a people of God. Jews in America cannot depend for their own spiritual vitality upon a vicarious, sentimental affinity for an independent, secular Jewish state. It must, in some way, fulfill the prophetic vision: ''For out of Zion shall go forth the law, and the word of the Lord from Jerusalem'' (Isaiah 2:3).

This mutual responsibility among Jews in America, Israel, and elsewhere is not just a theoretical proposition for public debate. It is a major building block for more intelligent and productive insights into the meaning of Jewish identity. The horizon of the American Jew is no longer limited by two oceans. It now encompasses the entire world. The merit of his contribution now depends on how far and how well he can sustain the echoes of Sinai against a formidable secular opposition.

Although the depth of his convictions and the quality of his Jewish life will depend upon his own deliberate initiative, as well as circumstances impossible to anticipate, the American Jew may still find inspiration in knowing that his Covenant with God has endured the best and worst of times. With sufficient faith and determination, it always will. If those inspired by its aspirations persist and persevere, Judaism will remain, in spite of any adversities, an eternal Covenant.

Suggestions for Further Reading

The following volumes are recommended as a helpful supplement to a fuller understanding and appreciation of Judaism in religious terms. The list is by no means an exhaustive collection of the available literature, but only a modest selection of sources designed to broaden and deepen an awareness of basic Jewish thought and practice.

Buber, Martin. *Hasidism.* New York: Philosophical Library, 1948.
A meticulous and thorough account of the major tenets of Hasidism by one of the leading theologians of the twentieth century, the author of the widely acclaimed *I-Thou, The Eclipse of God* and *Tales of the Hasidim,* who considered the truths of Hasidism to be extremely vital for Jews and Christians.

Cohen, Henry. *Why Judaism?* New York: Union of American Hebrew Congregations, 1973.
A general survey of Jewish thought and practice which delineates thematically many of the questions most frequently asked about Judaism and Jewish life. The book addresses subjects from Jewish views about God to definitions of the bonds between American Jews and Israel.

Davis, Moshe. *Emergence of Conservative Judaism.* Philadelphia: Jewish Publication Society of America, 1963.
A systematic treatment of the origins and developments of Conservative Judaism in America beginning with its roots in Europe and continuing to its current status as the largest Jewish religious movement in the United States.

Donin, Hayim. *To Be a Jew: A Guide to Jewish Observance in Comtemporary thought.* New York: Basic Books, 1972.
A presentation of traditional Jewish practice selected and compiled from the *Shulhan Aruk* (the authoritative source for Orthodox Jewish living) and the *Responsa* literature. Provides a rationale for the laws and traditions of Judaism.

Eban, Abba. *My Country.* New York: Random House, 1972.
A description of Israel's early struggles for security, the drama of mass immigration and absorption, the strains of economic crisis and consolidation, the revolutionary and cultural efforts to forge a new nation and a new self-image for an ancient people, and the frustrations that hampered all these efforts.

Elon, Amos. *The Israelis: Founders and Sons.* New York: Holt, Rinehart & Winston, 1971.

A penetrating analysis of the Israelis by a native son which explains the character of Israel with acute insight and unusual objectivity.

Fackenheim, Emil. *Encounters between Judaism and Modern Philosophy.* New York: Basic Books, 1973.

An examination of the main works of modern philosophy for the purpose of evaluating their contribution to contemporary life and to the vitality of Judaism. It is a major work of contemporary philosophy and a challenging preface to future Jewish thought.

Freehof, Solomon B. *Preface to Scripture.* New York: Union of American Hebrew Congregations, 1957.

A highly respected volume intended as a popular introduction to the Hebrew Bible for the lay person. Each Biblical book is presented with a concise descriptive outline stressing the significance of its main ideas, followed by a mosaic of verses which convey the message of the text. Each section also concludes with a commentary on every group of selected verses.

Glatzer, Nahum. *Hammer on the Rock: A Midrash Reader.* New York: Schocken Books, 1962.

A collection of literary materials from the non-legal parts of the Talmud, the Aggadah and the Midrashic writings, which provides succinct, imaginative, eloquent examples of Talmudic-Midrashic thinking and living; each selection suggests a broader vision and a wider range of implication.

Heschel, Abraham Joshua. *God in Search of Man.* Philadelphia: Jewish Publication Society of America, 1956.

A classic work which rediscovers categories of Biblical thinking, to establish their relevance and validity and shows how a Jewish understanding of the original Biblical way of thinking enables us to accept the reality of God.

Kaplan, Mordecai Menahem. *Judaism as a Civilization: Toward a Reconstruction of American-Jewish Life.* New York: The Reconstructionist Press, 1957.

The inspirational source for the ideological origins of the Reconstructionist movement conceived and developed by Mordecai M. Kaplan, a major Jewish theologian of the twentieth century. First published in 1944, this seminal work concentrates on the synthesis between Jewish tradition and modernism as a consequence of viewing Judaism in terms of a total civilization.

Kaufman, Yehezkel. *The Religion of Israel.* Chicago: University of Chicago Press, 1960.

A major contribution to Biblical scholarship and an abridgment of the original work in Hebrew which rests upon a fundamental evaluation of classical criticism and asserts that the Torah is the literary product of the earliest stage of Israelite religion, the one prior to literary prophecy.

Laqueur, Walter. *History of Zionism.* New York: Holt, Rinehart & Winston, 1972.

The first complete, general history of Zionism in English beginning with an account of its European background and continuing to the establishment of Israel. Sympathetic but not polemical. May well become the standard work in its field.

Martin, Bernard. *Prayer in Judaism.* New York: Basic Books, 1968.

Translations of nearly fifty of the most important Jewish prayers from a wide range of Jewish devotional literature, each of which is accompanied by an interpretative commentary, focusing on the historical background of the text, its religious meaning and its application for today.

Millgram, Abraham E. *Jewish Worship.* 2d ed. Philadelphia: Jewish Publication Society of America, 1975.

A comprehensive study of Jewish liturgy and prayer as expressions of rabbinic Judaism. Emphasis placed on the history and content of the *Siddur*, or prayer book, for Sabbaths and weekdays.

Moore, George Foot. *Judaism.* 3 vols. Cambridge: Harvard University Press, 1944.

Originally published in 1904 and republished several times by Schocken Books as a paperback. A classic multi-volume work tracing the development of Judaism during the rabbinic period. Based on primary sources, the author succeeds in clarifying the major components of Judaism which evolved during its most critical formative stages.

Neusner, Jacob. *Understanding American Judaism.* 2 vols. New York: Ktav Publishing House, 1975.

An anthology on American Judaism as a religion with special consideration for the religious forms, institutions, types of leadership and movements in which Judaism in America takes shape.

Orlinsky, Harry. *Ancient Israel.* Ithaca: Cornell University Press, 1954.

One of the first and finest investigations into the significance of the archaeological discoveries in Israel and the Near East and its implications for understanding Biblical society and the growth of the Biblical tradition.

Schauss, Hayim. *The Jewish Festivals.* Cincinnati: Union of American Hebrew Congregations, 1938.

A unique treatment not only of the historical and ceremonial significance of each of the Jewish festivals and fast days but of their changing observances and celebration throughout the centuries.

Scholem, Gershom. *Major Trends in Jewish Mysticism.* New York: Schocken Books, 1941.

The standard basic text for understanding Jewish mysticism with an elucidation of the function which this subject has served at varying periods, its ideals and its approach to the problems arising from the actual conditions of the time.

Seltzer, Robert M. *Jewish People, Jewish Thought: The Jewish Experience in*

History. New York: Macmillan Publishing Company, 1980.
A comprehensive overview of Jewish social and political history brilliantly integrated with the history of intellectual, religious and cultural traditions in one thorough, encyclopedic volume; enhanced by 200 illustrations, maps, chronological charts and an up-to-date bibliography for further reading. Covers every aspect of Judaism's encounter with continuously changing environment from Biblical times to the present.

Sklare, Marshal. *America's Jews*. New York: Random House, 1971.
A study by one of American Jewry's leading sociologists on the origins and experiences, the cultural patterns and social relationships of American Jews; he compares their situation with other ethnic groups who are frequently, if unfairly, measured by and against Jewish norms.

Steinberg, Milton. *Basic Judaism*. New York: Harcourt, Brace & World, 1947.
A distinguished contribution to an understanding of the essential teachings of Judaism, brilliantly formulated with clarity, brevity and simplicity.

Trapp, Leo. *A History of the Jewish Experience*. New York: Behrman House, 1973.
A treatment of the ideas of Judaism in the context of its historical framework based on the premise that Judaism is essentially a religion of reason and that Jewish history bears out this assertion.

Zeitlin, Solomon. *The Rise and Fall of the Judean State*. 2 vols. Philadelphia: The Jewish Publication Society of America, 1962.
A systematic history of the Judean state from 332 B.C.E. to 135 C.E., recounting the struggle for independence and detailing the origin and progress of the civil wars which eventually led to the destruction of the Second Commonwealth. Also treats extensively the rise and development of the Pharisees and their conflicts with the Sadducees. A fascinating account of Jewish sovereignty and its impact on the character of Jewish religious ideals.

Index

Index prepared by Micah D. Greenstein